Unit Resource Guide
Unit 3
Pennies, Pockets, and Parts

THIRD EDITION

KENDALL/HUNT PUBLISHING COMPANY
4050 Westmark Drive   Dubuque, Iowa 52002

A TIMS® Curriculum
University of Illinois at Chicago

UIC The University of Illinois
at Chicago

The original edition was based on work supported by the National Science Foundation under grant No. MDR 9050226 and the University of Illinois at Chicago. Any opinions, findings, and conclusions or recommendations expressed in this publication are those of the author(s) and do not necessarily reflect the views of the granting agencies.

1 2 3 4 5 6 7 8 9 10   11 10 09 08 07

Letter Home

Pennies, Pockets, and Parts

Date: _____

Dear Family Member:

Your child has been using numbers for counting and measuring. Now, your child will learn that numbers can be made from different combinations. For example, ten can be made from four and six and also from seven and three. As we explore numbers, your child will use connecting cubes and pennies to help solve problems.

Provide practice at home by:

- Encouraging your child to count and tally objects. Your child can tally road signs, trees, or houses on the street.

- Looking for quantities of ten as a whole and numbers less than ten as parts of a whole. For example, there are ten bowling pins and your child may only knock down four, or there are ten cars parked on the street and three are red.

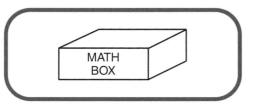

Create a math box to store counters.

Your efforts at home will strengthen your child's understanding of the math concepts explored at school. You can help your child by providing a box to store simple math materials, such as coins and beans, to help solve problems.

Your child will use pennies for a variety of activities in this unit. If possible, please send twenty-five pennies to add to our class bank.

Sincerely,

_____

Carta al hogar

Monedas, bolsillos y partes

Fecha: _____

Estimado miembro de familia:

Su hijo/a ha estado usando números para contar y medir. Ahora, su hijo/a aprenderá que los números pueden obtenerse a través de varias combinaciones. Por ejemplo, el diez puede obtenerse sumando cuatro y seis, y también sumando siete y tres. Mientras exploramos los números, su hijo/a usará cubos que se conectan y monedas de un centavo como ayuda para resolver problemas.

Ayude a su hijo/a en casa:

- Animándole a que cuente objetos. Su hijo/a puede contar señales de tránsito, árboles o casas por la calle.
- Buscando cantidades totales de diez unidades y números menores de diez que sean parte del total. Por ejemplo, hay diez bolos y su hijo/a puede derribar cuatro; o hay diez automóviles estacionados en la calle y tres son rojos.

Prepare una caja de matemáticas para guardar objetos para contar.

La práctica en casa reforzará la comprensión de los conceptos matemáticos explorados en la escuela. Puede ayudar a su hijo/a dándole una caja para que guarde materiales simples, como monedas y frijoles, que pueda usar para resolver problemas matemáticos.

Su hijo/a usará monedas de un centavo para distintas actividades en esta unidad. Si es posible, le pedimos que envíe veinticinco monedas de un centavo para agregarlas a la alcancía de la clase.

Atentamente,

_____

Table of Contents

Unit 3
Pennies, Pockets, and Parts

Outline 2

Background 9

Observational Assessment Record 11

Daily Practice and Problems 13

Lesson 1 *Favorite Colors* 24

Lesson 2 *Ten Frames* 32

Lesson 3 *Think and Spin* 42

Lesson 4 *Pockets Graph* 47

Lesson 5 *Pocket Parts* 52

Lesson 6 *What's in That Pocket?* 68

Lesson 7 *Purchasing with Pennies* 80

Glossary 87

Unit 3

Outline

Pennies, Pockets, and Parts

Estimated Class Sessions
15

Unit Summary

Work with numbers is extended to partitioning. The part-whole relationship is the basis for developing a strong understanding of addition and subtraction and is useful in learning basic facts. Ten frames provide a visual framework for number relationships, emphasizing the use of 5 and 10 as anchors. One primary context of the work is data collection and interpretation. There is also a strong problem-solving orientation to all aspects of the work.

Major Concept Focus

- tally marks
- gathering and recording data in tables and graphs
- ten frames
- exploring relationships among numbers
- using 5 and 10 as benchmarks
- number sentences
- partitioning a number in two or three parts
- word problems
- mathematical communication skills

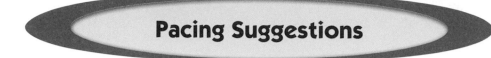

Pacing Suggestions

Unit 3 introduces mathematical concepts that will be revisited many times throughout the year. Use the recommended number of class sessions for each lesson as a guide for moving through the unit.

- Lesson 1 *Favorite Colors* and Lesson 4 *Pockets Graph* use data tables and bar graphs, two of the four components of the TIMS Laboratory Method. The complete method is used in Unit 5, so it is not necessary to focus on the other components here.

- Lesson 5 *Pocket Parts* introduces a variety of problem types. Students will solve problems in different ways that are meaningful to them. This is particularly important in Part 3 of the lesson, which challenges students to think about missing addend problems. Some students may be ready for this type of problem while others may not. Since this is only an introduction, move on after the allotted number of days.

- This is an appropriate time to begin collecting samples of student work for portfolios. See this unit's Background and the TIMS Tutor: *Portfolios* in the *Teacher Implementation Guide* for more information.

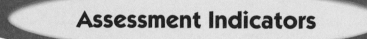

Assessment Indicators

Use the following Assessment Indicators and the *Observational Assessment Record* that follows the Background section in this unit to assess students on key ideas.

A1. Can students identify a number represented on a ten frame?

A2. Can students translate between representations of numbers (ten frames, tallies, manipulatives, and symbols)?

A3. Can students count on to solve addition problems?

A4. Can students partition a number into two and three parts?

A5. Can students solve addition problems and explain their reasoning?

A6. Can students use manipulatives to solve problems?

Unit Planner

	Lesson Information	Supplies	Copies/Transparencies
Lesson 1 **Favorite Colors** URG Pages 24–32 SG Pages 32–33 DPP A–B *Estimated Class Sessions* **1**	**Activity** Students generate and record data in a group data table. They keep track of totals with tally marks. **Math Facts Strategies** DPP item B develops counting strategies for the addition and subtraction facts. **Homework** 1. Students complete the *Kitchen Tools* Homework Page. 2. Students complete the *House Walk* Homework Page. **Assessment** 1. Use DPP item B to assess number sense. 2. Use Assessment Indicator A2 and the *Observational Assessment Record* to note students' abilities to translate between tallies and numbers.	• 1 self-adhesive note per student • group data table on easel paper	• 1 copy of *Observational Assessment Record* URG Pages 11–12 to be used throughout this unit
Lesson 2 **Ten Frames** URG Pages 32–41 SG Pages 35–39 DPP C–H *Estimated Class Sessions* **3**	**Activity** Students visualize numbers using five and ten as benchmarks. **Math Facts Strategies** DPP item C focuses on number patterns used in counting-on and counting-back strategies. **Assessment** 1. Students complete the *What's My Sentence?* Assessment Page. 2. Use Assessment Indicators A1, A2, and A5 and the *Observational Assessment Record* to document students' abilities to use ten frames as a tool to represent numbers and addition situations.	• 15 counters such as beans or pennies per student and teacher	• 1 transparency of *Ten Frames* SG Page 35
Lesson 3 **Think and Spin** URG Pages 42–46 SG Pages 41–45 DPP I–J *Estimated Class Sessions* **1**	**Activity** Students write number sentences that fit ten frames. **Homework** Send home the *Wearing Pockets* Homework Page that asks students to wear clothing with pockets for the next math class. **Assessment** Use Asssessment Indicator A2 and the *Observational Assessment Record* to document students' abilities to translate between representations of numbers (ten frames and symbols).	• 1 clear spinner per student pair and 1 for the teacher • 2 crayons, markers, or colored pencils per student pair	• 1 transparency of *Think and Spin* SG Page 41 • 1 transparency of *Ten Frame Recording Sheet* SG Page 43

	Lesson Information	**Supplies**	**Copies/ Transparencies**
Lesson 4 **Pockets Graph** URG Pages 47–51 DPP K–N *Estimated Class Sessions* **2**	**Activity** Students collect data and create a group bar graph.	• 12 connecting cubes per student • 1 self-adhesive note per student • group graph on easel paper	
Lesson 5 **Pocket Parts** URG Pages 52–67 SG Pages 47–53 DPP O–V *Estimated Class Sessions* **4**	**Activity** Students solve problems and write number sentences based on the number of pockets in each problem. **Math Facts Strategies** Each activity in this lesson provides opportunities for students to develop and practice math facts strategies. DPP item V reviews counting on and counting back. **Homework** Use the *More Pocket Parts 1* and *More Pocket Parts 2* Blackline Masters to construct homework pages. **Assessment** 1. Student complete the *Pockets* Assessment Page. 2. Use the *More Pocket Parts 1* or the *More Pocket Parts 2* Blackline Masters to develop a short assessment. 3. Use Assessment Indicators A3 and A6 and the *Observational Assessment Record* to document students' abilities to use manipulatives and the counting-on strategy to solve addition problems.	• 30 connecting cubes (10 cubes in 3 colors) per student • easel paper for a five-column data table or 1 transparency of *Five-column Data Table* URG Page 64	• copies of *More Pocket Parts 1* URG Page 62, prepared to create extra problems • copies of *More Pocket Parts 2* URG Page 63, prepared to create extra problems • 1 transparency of *Shirt, Pants, and Coat Pockets* URG Page 61 • 1 transparency of *Hidden Pockets* SG Page 52
Lesson 6 **What's in That Pocket?** URG Pages 68–79 SG Pages 55–63 DPP W–BB *Estimated Class Sessions* **3**	**Activity** Students partition numbers into two and three parts using pennies. They record their data in a table. **Math Facts Strategies** DPP items X, Y, AA, and BB review addition facts strategies. DPP item W reviews counting patterns necessary for counting on and counting back. **Homework** Assign the *Eight Pennies Data Table* Homework Page.	• 10 pennies per student and teacher • 1 blank transparency	• 1 copy of *Ten Frames* URG Page 76 per student

(Continued)

Lesson Information	Supplies	Copies/Transparencies

Assessment
1. Students complete the *Nine Pennies Data Table* Assessment Page.
2. Use DPP item Y as an assessment.
3. Use Assessment Indicators A2 and A4 and the *Observational Assessment Record* to document students' abilities to partition numbers and translate their work into addition number sentences.

Lesson 7

Purchasing with Pennies

URG Pages 80–85
SG Pages 35 and 65
DPP CC–DD

Estimated Class Sessions
1

Activity
Students solve story problems using pennies and price tags to "purchase" items in a classroom store. They explore multiple strategies for finding solutions.

Math Facts Strategies
DPP items CC and DD practice addition math facts strategies within the context of money in pockets.

Homework
Students complete the *What Would I Buy?* Homework Page.

Assessment
1. Use Assessment Indicators A3, A5, and A6 and the *Observational Assessment Record* to document students' abilities to solve addition problems using different strategies and to explain their reasoning.
2. Transfer appropriate documentation from the *Observational Assessment Record* to students' *Individual Assessment Record Sheets.*

Supplies:
• 10 pennies or other counters per student

Copies/Transparencies:
• 1 copy of *Ten Frames* URG Page 76 per student, optional
• 1 copy of *Individual Assessment Record Sheet* TIG Assessment section per student, previously copied for use throughout the year

---

Preparing for Upcoming Lessons

Remind students to wear clothes with pockets for Lessons 4 and 5. Send home the parent note in Lesson 3 reminding parents to have their children wear clothes with pockets to school.

In Lesson 7, each child will need pennies. Begin a class bank so students can help you collect pennies.

Connections

A current list of literature and software connections is available at *www.mathtrailblazers.com.* You can also find information on connections in the *Teacher Implementation Guide* Literature List and Software List sections.

Literature Connections
Suggested Titles

- Aker, Suzanne. *What Comes in 2's, 3's, and 4's?* Simon and Schuster, New York, 1992.
- Carle, Eric. *The Very Hungry Caterpillar.* Publishers' Group West, Berkeley, CA, 1994.
- Caudill, Rebecca. *A Pocketful of Cricket.* Holt, Rinehart and Winston, New York, 1999.
- Freeman, Don. *A Pocket for Corduroy.* The Viking Press, New York, 1999.

- Langstaff, John. *Over in the Meadow.* Harcourt, Brace, Jovanovich, New York, 1992.
- Payne, Emmy. *Katy No-Pocket.* Houghton Mifflin Company, Boston, 1999.
- Walsh, Ellen S. *Mouse Count.* Harcourt, Brace, Jovanovich, New York, 1999.

Software Connections

- *Math Concepts One . . . Two . . . Three!* provides practice with number sense, addition and subtraction with manipulatives and money, sorting two- and three-dimensional objects to find the symmetrical half, and making simple bar graphs.
- *Mighty Math Carnival Countdown* provides practice with identifying, counting, adding and subtracting money, and explores shapes, patterns, symmetry, area, perimeter, and fractions using pattern blocks.
- *Sunbuddy Math Playhouse* is a memory game involving counting, tallies, and analog and digital clocks.
- *Trudy's Time & Place House* explores time, the calendar, maps, directions, and geography.

Teaching All Math Trailblazers Students

Math Trailblazers® lessons are designed for students with a wide range of abilities. The lessons are flexible and do not require significant adaptation for diverse learning styles or academic levels. However, when needed, lessons can be tailored to allow students to engage their abilities to the greatest extent possible while building knowledge and skills.

To assist you in meeting the needs of all students in your classroom, this section contains information about some of the features in the curriculum that allow all students access to mathematics. For additional information, see the Teaching the *Math Trailblazers* Student: Meeting Individual Needs section in the *Teacher Implementation Guide.*

Differentiation Opportunities in this Unit

Games

Use games to promote or extend understanding of math concepts and to practice skills with children who need more practice.

- *Think and Spin* from Lesson 3 *Think and Spin*

Extensions

Use extensions to enrich lessons. Many extensions provide opportunities to further involve or challenge students of all abilities. Take a moment to review the extensions prior to beginning this unit. Some extensions may require additional preparation and planning. The following lessons contain extensions:

- Lesson 2 *Ten Frames*
- Lesson 6 *What's in That Pocket?*

Unit 3

Background
Pennies, Pockets, and Parts

Basic Number Concepts

Students extend their work with numbers to partitioning numbers, i.e., identifying parts of a whole. They learn, for example, that ten is five plus five; three plus seven; four plus four plus two; and so on. The concept of the part-whole relationship helps children develop more mature number sense, a better understanding of addition and subtraction, and strategies for the basic facts. Although students will be working informally with addition and subtraction concepts, do not focus on the operations or on computation.

Ten frames, which are introduced in this unit, are frequently recommended for primary grade mathematics instruction (Thompson, 1990; Thornton, 1990). Ten frames foster mental imagery based on five and ten that can help students build understanding of basic number concepts. Work with ten frames also provides a foundation for later developing fluency with the addition and subtraction math facts.

Research supports an approach to learning the facts that emphasizes the use of strategies to find answers over rote memorization of facts. As stated in *Mathematics for the Young Child,* "Encouraging children to use efficient strategies to derive unknown facts before drill is better than 'premature drill' and doing so increases both initial learning and retention." (Thornton, 1990)

Problem Solving

In this unit, data collection and analysis provide rich problem-solving contexts. There is evidence that young children bring to school a wealth of informal mathematical knowledge and strong problem-solving capabilities. This suggests that children are able to solve many kinds of problems in familiar contexts, particularly when they can use manipulatives, drawings, and their own ways of thinking.

"When the teaching and learning of mathematics is approached from a problem-solving perspective, concepts and procedural skills are developed on the basis of problem settings that require those concepts and skills. A problem-solving approach helps young children make sense of the concepts, skills, and relationships that are essential in an early childhood mathematics curriculum." (Worth, 1990)

It is important that students encounter a range of different kinds of problems. The work of Thomas Carpenter and his colleagues (Carpenter, Fennema, and Peterson, 1987; Carpenter, Carey, and Kouba, 1990) with the Cognitively Guided Instruction Project (CGI) provides insights that can help teachers with this process. They devised a classification scheme for problems most adults would solve by addition, subtraction, multiplication, or division. CGI classifies the addition and subtraction situations into 11 types of problems. Research by the CGI Project and others has shown that certain types of problems are more challenging than others. Traditionally, just two of the 11 addition and subtraction types have dominated elementary mathematics textbooks in the United States. Moreover, these favored problem types are the easiest to solve.

Most of the addition problems that elementary students encounter are classified as "join—result unknown." (For example, there are three corn plants in one row and two plants in another row. How many plants are there?) Similarly, most of the subtraction problems are "separate—result unknown." (For example, a farmer had 8 carrots and a rabbit ate 6 of them. How many carrots did the farmer have left?) With such a limited variety of problems, students develop a limited conception of addition and subtraction.

In Lesson 5 of this unit, students solve problems with missing parts, where the change or the start is unknown. (For example, Erika has five pockets altogether on her shirt and pants. She has two pockets on her shirt. How many pockets does she have on her pants?)

The TIMS Tutor: *Word Problems* reviews the research on addition and subtraction problem types and the wide variety of informal strategies children commonly use to solve them. (Carpenter and Moser, 1984; Carpenter, Carey, and Kouba, 1990)

Children must be allowed sufficient time to solve problems in their own ways. The opportunity to share mathematical thinking is crucial in creating a classroom climate in which children explore, think, and share to build their own knowledge.

Here is an example of two unique approaches to solving a problem.

> Problem: Melinda has five pennies and Carlos has ten pennies. How many more pennies does Carlos have?
>
> Child A: Makes two stacks, one of five cubes and the other of ten cubes, and places them next to each other. Then, counts the number of additional cubes in the taller stack.
>
> Child B: Makes two stacks, one of five cubes and the other of ten cubes. Then, indicates that five and five is ten.

It is important to nurture children's abilities and interest in problem solving, both by posing problems and by allowing them to create and solve their own problems.

Portfolios: Assessing Growth Over Time

As students write and solve problems, this is an appropriate time to start collecting samples of their work that can be kept in a portfolio. This collection shows how a student's skills, attitudes, or understandings grow over time. Artists and business people also use portfolios to show their strengths. Students can add to their portfolios throughout the year to record their progress. Portfolios allow students to see the mathematics they have learned while helping them identify their strengths and weaknesses. See the TIMS Tutor: *Portfolios* in the *Teacher Implementation Guide* for additional information.

Resources

- Carpenter, T.P., D.A. Carey, and V.L. Kouba. "A Problem-Solving Approach to the Operations." In *Mathematics for the Young Child,* J.N. Payne (Ed.). National Council of Teachers of Mathematics, Reston, VA, 1990.

- Carpenter, T.P., E. Fennema, M.L. Franke, L. Levi, and S.E. Empson. *Children's Mathematics: Cognitively Guided Instruction.* Heinemann, Westport, CT, 1999.

- Carpenter, T.P., E. Fennema, and P. Peterson. "Cognitively Guided Instruction: The Application of Cognitive and Instructional Science to Mathematics Curriculum Development." In *Developments in School Mathematics Education around the World.* I. Wirszup and R.R. Streit (Eds.). National Council of Teachers of Mathematics, Reston, VA, 1987.

- Carpenter, T.P., and J.M. Moser. "The Acquisition of Addition and Subtraction Concepts in Grades One through Three." *Journal for Research in Mathematics Education,* 15 (3), 1984.

- Thompson, C.S. "Place Value and Larger Numbers." In *Mathematics for the Young Child.* J.N. Payne (Ed.). National Council of Teachers of Mathematics, Reston, VA, 1990.

- Thornton, C.A. "Strategies for the Basic Facts." In *Mathematics for the Young Child.* J.N. Payne (Ed.). National Council of Teachers of Mathematics, Reston, VA, 1990.

- Worth, Joan. "Developing Problem-Solving Abilities and Attitudes." In *Mathematics for the Young Child,* J.N. Payne (Ed.). National Council of Teachers of Mathematics, Reston, VA, 1990.

Observational Assessment Record

(A1) Can students identify a number represented on a ten frame?

(A2) Can students translate between representations of numbers (ten frames, tallies, manipulatives, and symbols)?

(A3) Can students count on to solve addition problems?

(A4) Can students partition a number into two and three parts?

(A5) Can students solve addition problems and explain their reasoning?

(A6) Can students use manipulatives to solve problems?

(A7) _____

Name	A1	A2	A3	A4	A5	A6	A7	Comments
1.								
2.								
3.								
4.								
5.								
6.								
7.								
8.								
9.								
10.								
11.								
12.								
13.								

Name	A1	A2	A3	A4	A5	A6	A7	Comments
14.								
15.								
16.								
17.								
18.								
19.								
20.								
21.								
22.								
23.								
24.								
25.								
26.								
27.								
28.								
29.								
30.								
31.								
32.								

Unit 3

Daily Practice and Problems
Pennies, Pockets, and Parts

A DPP Menu for Unit 3

Two Daily Practice and Problems (DPP) items are included for each class session listed in the Unit Outline. A scope and sequence chart for the DPP is in the *Teacher Implementation Guide.*

Icons in the Teacher Notes column designate the subject matter of each DPP item. Each item falls into one or more of the categories listed below. A menu of the DPP items for Unit 3 follows.

N Number Sense	Computation	Time	Geometry
A–C, F–H, V, W, Z	I, J, P	H–J, P–S	D, E, K–O, T, U
Math Facts Strategies	$ Money	Measurement	Data
B, C, V–Y, AA–DD	X, Y, AA–DD	F, G	Z

Students may solve the items individually, in groups, or as a class. The items may also be assigned for homework. The DPPs are also available on the Teacher Resource CD.

Student Questions	Teacher Notes
A More or Less 1 	Repeat with 5 cubes.
I will place a number of cubes on the overhead. I will flash the light on and off. Tell me if there are more or less than ten cubes on the overhead. How did you decide?	
B What Number?	
1. What number follows five?	1. 6
	2. 4
	3. 9
	4. 7
2. What number comes just before five?	
3. What number follows eight?	
4. What number comes just before eight?	

Student Questions	Teacher Notes
C **What Number Again?** 1. What number follows seven? 2. What number comes just before seven? 3. What number follows nine? 4. What number comes just before nine?	**1. 8** **2. 6** **3. 10** **4. 8**
D **Making Shapes 1** Place a red trapezoid pattern block on the overhead. How can you make this trapezoid using other pattern blocks?	**Use 3 triangles or 1 blue rhombus and 1 triangle.**
E **Making Shapes 2** Place a blue rhombus on the overhead. How can you make this rhombus shape using other pattern blocks?	**Use 2 triangles.**

F **More or Less 2**

1. Find two objects in the classroom that are close to twelve links long.

2. Find two objects that are less than twelve links long.

3. Find two objects that are more than twelve links long.

Hold up a chain of twelve links for children to use as a reference or have children build their own chains.

G **More or Less 3**

1. Find two objects in the classroom that are close to four links long.

2. Find two objects that are less than four links long.

3. Find two objects that are more than four links long.

H **Calendar Count 1**

The numbers fell off our classroom calendar. Help me number the days of the month.

I **Calendar Count 2**

Kenji's birthday is on the ninth day of this month. Melissa's birthday is two weeks later. What is the date of Melissa's birthday?

Show students a calendar.

Student Questions	Teacher Notes

J **Calendar Count 3**

☒ ⌛

Labor Day is on a Monday. Henrique's birthday is two weeks later.

Show students a calendar.

1. On what day of the week is Henrique's birthday?

2. What is the date for Henrique's birthday?

K **How Many Shapes 1?**

Place a blue rhombus and six green triangles on the overhead. How many blue rhombuses can you make with these triangles?

3 rhombuses

L **How Many Shapes 2?**

Place a yellow hexagon and six blue rhombuses on the overhead. How many hexagons can you make with these blue rhombuses?

2 hexagons

Student Questions	Teacher Notes
M How Many Shapes 3? Place a yellow hexagon and six red trapezoids on the overhead. How many hexagons can you make with these trapezoids?	3 hexagons
N What Do You Know About Triangles? List all the things we know about triangles.	Class brainstorms and teacher records statements on the overhead.
O What Do You Know About Squares? List all the things we know about squares.	Class brainstorms and teacher records statements on the overhead.
P Calendar Count 4 1. Today is ____. (Date) In eleven days it will be ____. 2. Today is ____. (Day) In eleven days it will be ____.	Show students a calendar.

Student Questions	Teacher Notes
Q **Calendar Count 5** 1. What are the names of the months? 2. How many months are in one year?	1. January, February, March, April, May, June, July, August, September, October, November, December 2. 12
R **Calendar Count 6** 1. What is the first month of the year? 2. What is the last month of the year?	1. January 2. December
S **Calendar Count 7** 1. In which month is your birthday? 2. Find another student who was born in the same month as you.	
T **What Do You Know About Rhombuses?** List all the things we know about rhombuses.	Class brainstorms and teacher records statements on the overhead.
U **What Do You Know About Hexagons?** List all the things we know about hexagons.	Class brainstorms and teacher records statements on the overhead.

Student Questions	Teacher Notes

V **What Number Once Again?**

$\begin{smallmatrix} 7 \\ +3 \end{smallmatrix}$ N

1. What number follows ten?

2. What number comes just before ten?

3. What number follows twelve?

4. What number comes just before twelve?

1. 11
2. 9
3. 13
4. 11

W **What Number Once More?**

$\begin{smallmatrix} 7 \\ +3 \end{smallmatrix}$ N

1. What number follows fifteen?

2. What number comes just before fifteen?

3. What number follows nineteen?

4. What number comes just before nineteen?

1. 16
2. 14
3. 20
4. 18

X **Penny Problems 1**

$ $ $\begin{smallmatrix} 7 \\ +3 \end{smallmatrix}$

You have ten pennies. Three pennies are in your shirt pocket. The rest are in your pants pocket. How many pennies are in your pants pocket?

7 pennies

Y **Penny Problems 2**

$ | $\frac{7}{+3}$

1. Sue found ten pennies in her pockets. Eight pennies were in her shirt pocket. How many were in her pants pocket?

2. Sue found eight pennies in her pockets. One penny was in a shirt pocket. Four pennies were in her pants pockets. How many were in her coat pocket?

Encourage students to use pennies to solve the problems and then write number sentences.

1. 8¢ + $\underline{2¢}$ = 10¢

2. 1¢ + 4¢ + $\underline{3¢}$ = 8¢

Z **Tallies**

T.J. has a shell collection. He listed all the colors of his shells: white, gray, white, tan, gray, gray, pink, gray, tan, pink, pink, gray, white, and gray. Use tallies to record the colors of T.J.'s shells in the table below.

Color	Tallies	Number
Pink		
Gray		
White		
Tan		

Then, write the number of shells for each color.

This item can be completed at the overhead or on the board. Call out each color as a student marks the tally.

Student Questions	Teacher Notes

AA Pennies

Emily has 6 pennies. Complete the table below to show different ways Emily can place her 6 pennies into 2 pockets. Then, write a number sentence for each.

Pocket 1	Pocket 2	Number Sentence
0¢	6¢	0¢ + 6¢ = 6¢

Some possible number sentences include:

0¢ + 6¢ = 6¢

1¢ + 5¢ = 6¢

2¢ + 4¢ = 6¢

3¢ + 3¢ = 6¢

BB More Pennies

Tyler has 5 pennies. Complete the table below to show different ways Tyler can place his 5 pennies into 3 pockets. Then, write a number sentence for each.

Pocket 1	Pocket 2	Pocket 3	Number Sentence
1¢	1¢	3¢	1¢ + 1¢ + 3¢ = 5¢

Some possible number sentences include:

0¢ + 0¢ + 5¢ = 5¢

1¢ + 1¢ + 3¢ = 5¢

2¢ + 2¢ + 1¢ = 5¢

4¢ + 1¢ + 0¢ = 5¢

CC Penny Problems 3

$ ⊞

1. You have 3¢. You want to buy a pencil. How many more pennies do you need?

2. You have 10¢. Do you have enough to buy a pencil, eraser, and folder?

Display a sticker, an eraser, a pencil, and a folder. Attach a large price tag to each. Label the sticker as 2¢, eraser 3¢, pencil 4¢, and the folder 5¢.

1. 1¢

2. No, you need 2¢ more.

DD Penny Problems 4

$ ⊞

1. You bought two things and spent 7¢. What did you buy? See if you can find more than one answer.

2. You have 9¢. What can you buy? See if you can find more than one answer.

See CC for prices of objects.

1. Eraser and pencil or folder and sticker.

2. Answers will vary. Some possible answers: folder and pencil, 3 erasers, etc.

Lesson 1

Favorite Colors

Lesson Overview

Estimated Class Sessions

1

Each student tells his or her favorite color. The class uses the information to make their first group data table. In a teacher-led discussion, students think and talk about their data.

Key Content

- Collecting, organizing, and analyzing data.
- Translating between representations of numbers (tallies and symbols).
- Communicating mathematics orally and in writing.

Key Vocabulary

- data table
- tally

Math Facts Strategies

DPP item B develops counting strategies for the addition and subtraction facts.

Homework

1. Students complete the *Kitchen Tools* Homework Page.
2. Students complete the *House Walk* Homework Page.

Assessment

1. Use DPP item B to assess number sense.
2. Use Assessment Indicator A2 and the *Observational Assessment Record* to note students' abilities to translate between tallies and numbers.

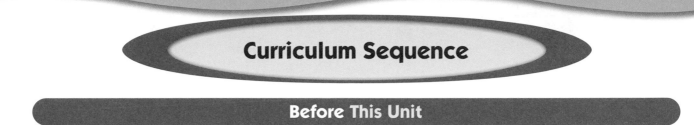

Curriculum Sequence

Before This Unit

Data Tables

Students used data tables in kindergarten as they looked for patterns in partitioning numbers. Students learned that a data table can be a useful tool in studying number relationships. See Data Collection: How Many, How Much, How Far? in the Ongoing Content section in the kindergarten *Teacher Resource Book*.

In Unit 2 of first grade, students began collecting and recording daily weather data in a table.

After This Unit

Data Tables

Work with data tables is included in Units 5, 6, 7, 8, 11, 16, and 19.

TIMS Laboratory Method

In Unit 5, students will be introduced to all four phases of the TIMS Laboratory Method as they collect, graph, and analyze data about the distribution of colored pieces in a box of cereal.

Materials List

Supplies and Copies

Student	Teacher
Supplies for Each Student • self-adhesive note	**Supplies** • group data table on easel paper
Copies	**Copies/Transparencies** • 1 copy of *Observational Assessment Record* to be used throughout this unit (*Unit Resource Guide* Pages 11–12)

All blackline masters including assessment, transparency, and DPP masters are also on the Teacher Resource CD.

Student Books
Kitchen Tools (*Student Guide* Page 32)
House Walk (*Student Guide* Page 33)

Daily Practice and Problems
DPP items A–B (*Unit Resource Guide* Page 14)

Assessment Tools
Observational Assessment Record (*Unit Resource Guide* Pages 11–12)

A. More or Less 1 (URG p. 14)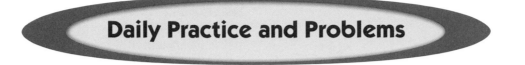

I will place a number of cubes on the overhead. I will flash the light on and off. Tell me if there are more or less than ten cubes on the overhead. How did you decide?

B. What Number? (URG p. 14)

1. What number follows five?
2. What number comes just before five?
3. What number follows eight?
4. What number comes just before eight?

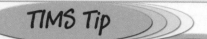
Before the Activity

Construct a data table as in Figure 1. Make sure that it is large enough to accommodate multiple self-adhesive notes in the "Names of Students" column.

Favorite Colors

Colors	Names of Students	Tallies	Total
Red			
Orange			
Yellow			
Pink			
Blue			
Purple			
Green			
Black			
Brown			
White			

Figure 1: *Favorite Colors Data Table*

Teaching the Activity

To generate the data, ask each student to choose a color from the chart.

Then demonstrate the value of organizing data in a table. Ask all students who chose red to stand. The rest of the group should count the students who are standing. Repeat this for other colors. After completing this process, ask questions such as these:

*   *Do you remember how many students chose yellow?*

*   *Can you tell us how many other students chose the same color as you?*

The questions can lead to uncertainty or confusion on the part of students. Remembering numbers without a visual record is difficult. Having just experienced this difficulty, students will be ready for the introduction of the data table, a tool for recording and organizing data.

Ask children to write their names on self-adhesive notes. Instruct those who chose red to bring their self-adhesive notes to the front. Students should put their notes on the data table in the "Names of Students" column. Continue with the remaining students and their favorite colors.

Read the names on the self-adhesive notes aloud. Make a tally mark for each name. Present the tally system, in which four marks are crossed by a fifth. This will help students see units of five and will create a background for skip counting by fives, which is introduced in a later unit. Ask children to count the number of tally marks and to write the total in the total column.

Discuss results in your data table. The following questions might aid your discussion:

- *How many students chose red as their favorite color?*
- *How many students chose blue?*
- *Which color did students choose the most?*
- *Which color did students choose the least?*
- *Are there any colors that the same number of children liked?*
- *What are they?*
- *How many colors did less than five people choose?*
- *How many colors did more than five people choose?*
- *Can you tell more than five and less than five from the tally marks?*
- *How many students chose green, black, and purple altogether?*
- *How many students chose red, yellow, and blue altogether?*

Math Facts Strategies

DPP item B develops counting strategies for the addition and subtraction facts.

Homework and Practice

- DPP item A uses benchmark numbers 5 and 10 to help students estimate.
- Assign the *Kitchen Tools* Homework Page. Students use tally marks to count objects.
- The *House Walk* Homework Page provides additional practice for using tally marks.

Assessment

- Use DPP item B to assess students' number sense.
- Use the *Observational Assessment Record* to note students' abilities to translate between tallies and numbers.

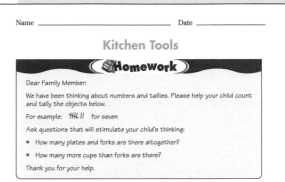

Name _____ Date _____

Kitchen Tools

Homework

Dear Family Member:

We have been thinking about numbers and tallies. Please help your child count and tally the objects below.

For example: ‖‖‖ II for seven

Ask questions that will stimulate your child's thinking:

* How many plates and forks are there altogether?
* How many more cups than forks are there?

Thank you for your help.

Count and tally the objects in the table.

Objects	Tallies	Total
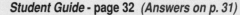		

SG • Grade 1 • Unit 3 • Lesson 1   Favorite Colors

Student Guide - page 32 (Answers on p. 31)

Name _____ Date _____

House Walk

Homework

Dear Family Member:

Please help your child count the objects listed in the table. As you go from room to room, have your child record a tally for each object he or she sees. After all of the rooms have been checked, have your child count the tallies and record the total.

Thank you for your cooperation.

Record a tally for each object in your home. Then, count the tallies and record the total.

Object	Tallies	Total
Lamp		
Chair		
Table		
Clock		
Window		

Favorite Colors   SG • Grade 1 • Unit 3 • Lesson 1

Student Guide - page 33 (Answers on p. 31)

At a Glance

Math Facts Strategies and Daily Practice and Problems

DPP item A uses the benchmark numbers 5 and 10 to help students estimate. Item B develops math facts strategies.

Teaching the Activity (A2)

1. Students choose a color from the table.
2. Students stand and count how many students selected each color without recording the data.
3. Discuss the importance of organizing and recording data in a table.
4. Students write their names on self-adhesive notes.
5. Students place the self-adhesive notes on the table next to their favorite color.
6. Make a tally mark for each name.
7. Students discuss the data.
8. Students answer questions about the data.

Homework

1. Students complete the *Kitchen Tools* Homework Page.
2. Students complete the *House Walk* Homework Page.

Assessment

1. Use DPP item B to assess number sense.
2. Use Assessment Indicator A2 and the *Observational Assessment Record* to note students' abilities to translate between tallies and numbers.

Answer Key is on page 31.

Notes:

Student Guide (p. 32)

Kitchen Tools

Objects	Tallies	Total
teacups	////	4
forks	///	3
plates	⅂⅂⅂⅂ ///	8
measuring cups	⅂⅂⅂⅂	5
spoons	//	2
glasses	⅂⅂⅂⅂ /	6

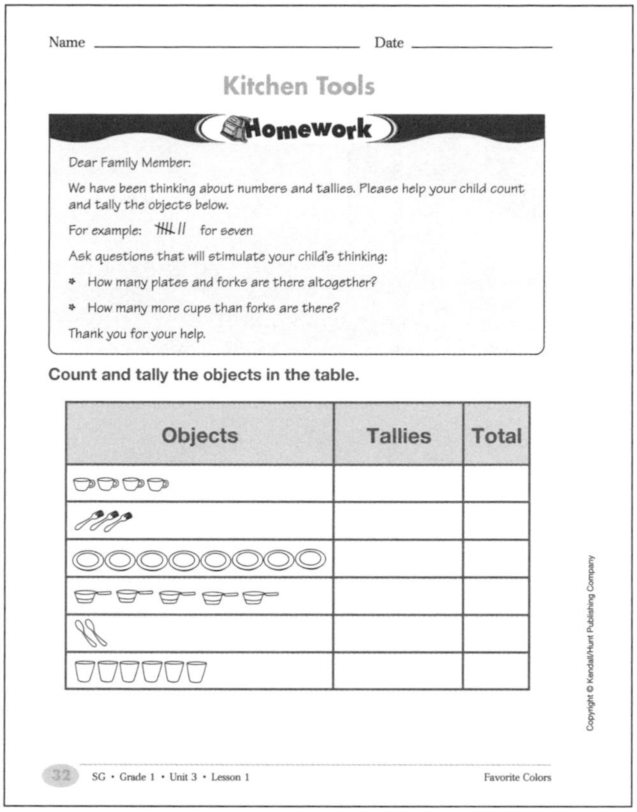

Student Guide - page 32

Student Guide (p. 33)

House Walk

Answers will vary.

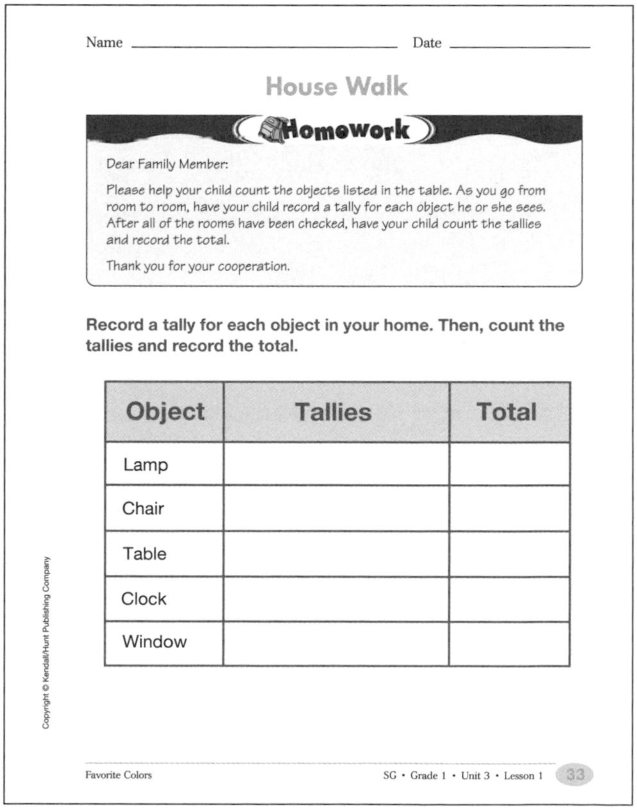

Student Guide - page 33

Lesson 2

Ten Frames

Lesson Overview

Estimated Class Sessions

3

Students learn to represent numbers on a ten frame (see Figure 2). The ten frame is a tool that helps students visualize numbers.

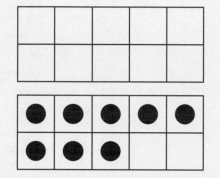

Figure 2: *On the top, an empty ten frame; on the bottom, the number eight*

Ten frame images are closely linked to the numbers five and ten. The representation of eight in Figure 2 shows that eight is three more than five and two less than ten.

Key Content

- Developing number sense using part-whole relationships.
- Visualizing numbers using five and ten as benchmarks.
- Identifying numbers represented on ten frames.
- Translating between different representations of numbers (ten frames and addition number sentences).
- Adding using ten frames and counters.

Math Facts Strategies

DPP item C focuses on number patterns used in counting-on and counting-back strategies.

Assessment

1. Students complete the *What's My Sentence?* Assessment Page.
2. Use Assessment Indicators A1, A2, and A5 and the *Observational Assessment Record* to document students' abilities to use ten frames as a tool to represent numbers and addition situations.

Curriculum Sequence

Before This Unit

Ten Frames

Students used ten frames in kindergarten as they counted the number of school days as part of the daily calendar work.

Number Sentences

Students were introduced to writing number sentences in conjunction with the ten frame in kindergarten.

After This Unit

Ten Frames

Students will continue to use ten frames to represent numbers and to solve problems. See Units 5, 8, 9, 11, and 13.

Materials List

Supplies and Copies

Student	Teacher
Supplies for Each Student • 15 counters, such as beans or pennies	**Supplies** • 15 counters, such as beans or pennies
Copies	**Copies/Transparencies** • 1 transparency of *Ten Frames* (*Student Guide* Page 35)

All blackline masters including assessment, transparency, and DPP masters are also on the Teacher Resource CD.

Student Books
Ten Frames (*Student Guide* Page 35)
What's My Number? (*Student Guide* Page 37)
Number Sentences (*Student Guide* Page 38)
What's My Sentence? (*Student Guide* Page 39)

Daily Practice and Problems
DPP items C–H (*Unit Resource Guide* Pages 15–16)

Assessment Tools
Observational Assessment Record (*Unit Resource Guide* Pages 11–12)

Daily Practice and Problems

Suggestions for using the DPPs are on page 38.

C. What Number Again? (URG p. 15) [N] [+3/7]

1. What number follows seven?
2. What number comes just before seven?
3. What number follows nine?
4. What number comes just before nine?

D. Making Shapes 1 (URG p. 15)

Place a red trapezoid pattern block on the overhead. How can you make this trapezoid using other pattern blocks?

E. Making Shapes 2 (URG p. 15)

Place a blue rhombus on the overhead. How can you make this rhombus shape using other pattern blocks?

F. More or Less 2 (URG p. 16) [N]

1. Find two objects in the classroom that are close to twelve links long.
2. Find two objects that are less than twelve links long.
3. Find two objects that are more than twelve links long.

G. More or Less 3 (URG p. 16) [N]

1. Find two objects in the classroom that are close to four links long.
2. Find two objects that are less than four links long.
3. Find two objects that are more than four links long.

H. Calendar Count 1 (URG p. 16) [N]

The numbers fell off our classroom calendar. Help me number the days of the month.

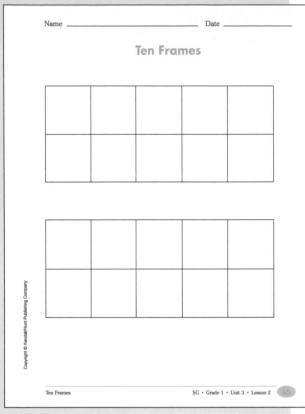

Name _____ Date _____

Ten Frames

Student Guide - page 35

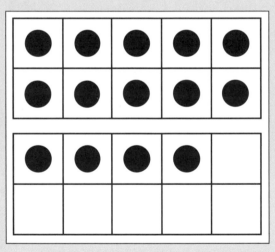

Figure 3: *Fourteen on two ten frames*

Teaching the Activity

Part 1 Introducing Ten Frames

Show a *Ten Frames* transparency on the overhead projector. Put counters in the ten frame by filling the top row left-to-right and then the bottom row left-to-right. Place counters in the ten frame to show a few numbers such as two, five, and seven so that children get the idea. Then place eight counters in the ten frame. Ask:

* *How can we figure out how many counters are on the ten frame?*

Some students may suggest:

* counting from one;
* counting on from five;
* that there are five counters in the top row and three more in the other row. So that makes eight altogether;
* that two counters are missing from the ten frame. Counting back from ten, the answer is eight.

Point out that eight is three more than five and is also two less than ten. Each time you show a number on the ten frame, emphasize the connections to five and ten.

After students are comfortable with numbers up to ten, introduce eleven through fifteen by starting a third row in a second ten frame. Figure 3 shows fourteen on two ten frames.

Part 2 Working with Ten Frames

Ask a volunteer to come to the overhead and show a number on the ten frame. The class can suggest numbers for the volunteers. Stress the connections to five and ten for each number.

> **TIMS Tip**
>
> Reemphasize left-to-right and top-to-bottom placement of counters to establish consistent visual imagery based on five and ten.

Now, students are ready to work on their own. Ask them to turn to the *Ten Frames* Activity Page. Give each student fifteen counters and numbers to show on their individual ten frames. As they work, observe to see if they are filling the ten frames as instructed.

> **TIMS Tip**
>
> Students may choose to use ten frames as tools for problem solving throughout the year. Make paper or laminated copies of the *Ten Frames* Activity Page available.

Ask students to complete the *What's My Number?* Activity Page. This may be used as an assessment or as homework. If possible, have students demonstrate the different strategies they used to solve the problems.

Part 3 Playing *Ten Frame Flash*

To play *Ten Frame Flash,* turn off the overhead projector. Place six counters on the *Ten Frames* transparency. Ask students to watch the screen while you flash the overhead on and off. Do not give children enough time to count since the objective is to learn to use the five and ten benchmarks. Ask:

* *How many counters did you see? How do you know?* (Turn the projector on again so they can see if they were correct.)

Repeat this for other numbers. When you think students are ready, introduce the numbers eleven through fifteen in the same manner.

Part 4 Number Sentences and Ten Frames

Top Row Plus Bottom Row. Place seven counters on the *Ten Frames* transparency. Ask:

* *How many counters are in the top row?* (5)
* *How many counters are in the other row?* (2)
* *How many counters are there altogether?* (7)

Encourage students to write sentences using words about the problems. Write on the board:

* *Five counters and two more counters equals seven counters.*

Ask:

* *I could also write a **number sentence** about this problem. What is a number sentence?* (A number sentence uses numbers and symbols instead of words. 5 + 2 = 7 is a number sentence.)
* *What does + mean?*
* *What does = mean?*

Repeat the activity above with numbers up to ten on the ten frame.

Filled Plus Empty. Place eight counters on the *Ten Frames* transparency. Ask:

* *How many counters are in the ten frame?* (8)
* *How many empty spaces are there?* (2)

Write a number sentence. (8 + 2 = 10)
Place three counters in the ten frame. Ask:

* *How many counters are in the ten frame?* (3)
* *How many empty spaces are there?* (7)
* *What is a number sentence for this problem?* (3 + 7 = 10)

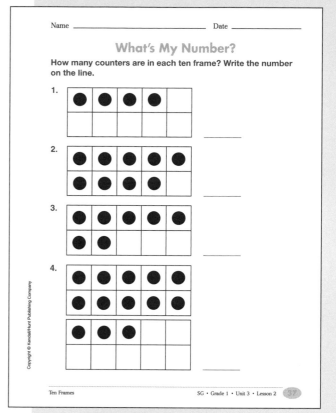

Student Guide - page 37 (Answers on p. 40)

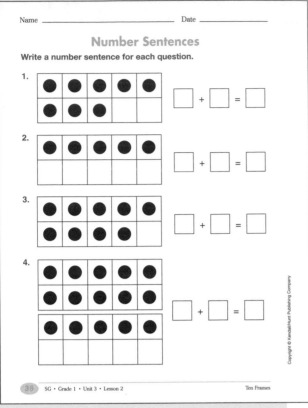
Student Guide - page 38 *(Answers on p. 40)*

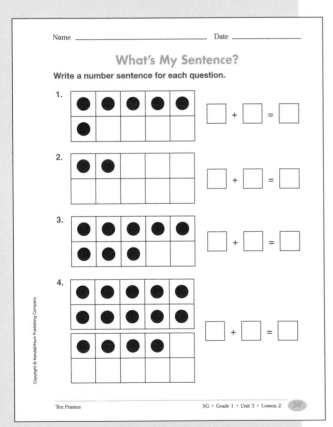
Student Guide - page 39 *(Answers on p. 41)*

Repeat the previous activity with different numbers on the ten frame. Ask students to compare the different number sentences. In each case, the total number of counters is ten.

Greater than Ten. Place thirteen counters on the *Ten Frames* transparency. Ask:

*   *How many counters are there?* (13)
*   *Give a number sentence for this ten frame.*
    (10 + 3 = 13)

Repeat this activity with numbers between ten and fifteen.

After your students are comfortable writing these number sentences, you may want them to investigate number sentences that total fifteen such as 14 + 1 = 15. (Fourteen counters plus one open spot equals fifteen.)

More than one number sentence can fit a given ten frame. Display a number on the ten frame and ask the class to list the number sentences that fit. The *Number Sentences* Activity Page provides additional practice.

Math Facts Strategies

DPP item C focuses on number patterns used in counting-on and counting-back strategies.

Homework and Practice

*   DPP items D and E review geometry concepts.
*   DPP items F and G compare measurements with links.
*   DPP item H uses the calendar as a context for developing counting skills.

Assessment

*   Students write number sentences representing partially filled ten frames on the *What's My Sentence?* Assessment Page.
*   Use the *Observational Assessment Record* to note students' progress in identifying numbers on ten frames, translating between ten frames and addition number sentences, and explaining their reasoning.

Extension

If students are ready, ask them to use the *Number Sentences* Activity Page to make subtraction sentences based on the ten frames. For example, one possible sentence for *Question 1* is 10 − 8 = 2.

At a Glance

Math Facts Strategies and Daily Practice and Problems

DPP item C focuses on counting strategies. DPP items D and E review geometry concepts. DPP items F and G use comparison language in a measurement context. DPP item H uses the calendar.

Part 1. Introducing Ten Frames

1. Show the *Ten Frames* transparency.
2. Place counters in the ten frame and ask how many there are.
3. Children share their strategies.
4. Repeat using different numbers. Each time you show a number on the ten frame, emphasize its connections to 5 and 10.

Part 2. Working with Ten Frames (A1)

1. Ask a volunteer to show a number on the ten frame.
2. Give students numbers to show on their *Ten Frames* Activity Page.
3. Students complete the *What's My Number?* Activity Page and discuss their strategies.

Part 3. Playing *Ten Frame Flash* (A1)

Place counters on the *Ten Frames* transparency. Flash the overhead on and off. Ask students to identify each number without counting.

Part 4. Number Sentences and Ten Frames (A2) (A5)

1. Students investigate number sentences based on five. (Top row plus the bottom row of a ten frame.)
2. Students investigate number sentences that add up to ten. (Filled squares plus empty squares.)
3. Students investigate number sentences in which the sum is ten.
4. Students compare number sentences in which the sum is ten.
5. Students investigate number sentences in which the sum is fifteen.
6. Students write a variety of number sentences for the same ten frame.
7. Students complete the *Number Sentences* Activity Page.

Assessment

1. Students complete the *What's My Sentence?* Assessment Page.
2. Use Assessment Indicators A1, A2, and A5 and the *Observational Assessment Record* to document students' abilities to use ten frames as a tool to represent numbers and addition situations.

Extension

Students use the *Number Sentences* Activity Page to make subtraction sentences based on ten frames.

Answer Key is on pages 40–41.

Notes:

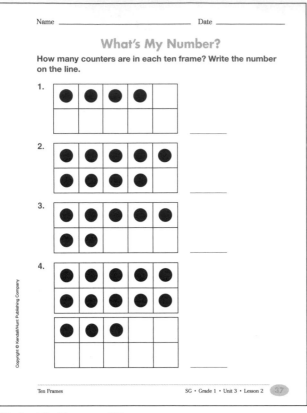

Student Guide - page 37

Student Guide (p. 37)

What's My Number?

1. 4

2. 9

3. 7

4. 13

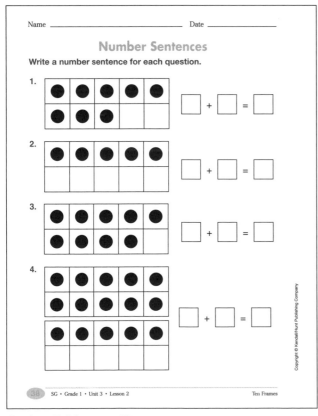

Student Guide - page 38

Student Guide (p. 38)

Number Sentences

Number sentences will vary. Some possible number sentences include:

1. $5 + 3 = 8$; $8 + 2 = 10$

2. $2 + 3 = 5$; $5 + 5 = 10$

3. $5 + 4 = 9$; $9 + 1 = 10$

4. $10 + 5 = 15$; $15 + 5 = 20$

Student Guide (p. 39)

What's My Sentence?

Number sentences will vary. Some possible number sentences include:

1. $5 + 1 = 6$; $6 + 4 = 10$
2. $2 + 0 = 2$; $1 + 1 = 2$; $2 + 8 = 10$
3. $5 + 3 = 8$; $8 + 2 = 10$
4. $10 + 4 = 14$; $14 + 1 = 15$; $14 + 6 = 20$

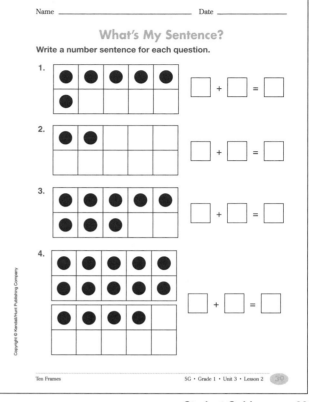

Student Guide - page 39

Lesson 3

Think and Spin

Lesson Overview

Students play a game using a spinner and a ten frame to make sums and record numbers less than ten. They then write a number sentence.

Key Content

- Translating between different representations of numbers.
- Writing addition number sentences.

Homework

Send home the *Wearing Pockets* Homework Page that asks students to wear clothing with pockets for the next math class.

Assessment

Use Assessment Indicator A2 and the *Observational Assessment Record* to document students' abilities to translate between representations of numbers (ten frames and symbols).

Supplies and Copies

Student	Teacher
Supplies for Each Student Pair • clear plastic spinner • 2 crayons, markers, or colored pencils	**Supplies** • clear plastic spinner
Copies	**Copies/Transparencies** • 1 transparency of *Think and Spin* (*Student Guide* Page 41) • 1 transparency of *Ten Frame Recording Sheet* (*Student Guide* Page 43)

All blackline masters including assessment, transparency, and DPP masters are also on the Teacher Resource CD.

Student Books

Think and Spin (*Student Guide* Page 41)
Ten Frame Recording Sheet (*Student Guide* Page 43)
Wearing Pockets (*Student Guide* Page 45)

Daily Practice and Problems

DPP items I–J (*Unit Resource Guide* Pages 16–17)

Assessment Tools

Observational Assessment Record (*Unit Resource Guide* Pages 11–12)

Daily Practice and Problems

Suggestions for using the DPPs are on page 45.

I. Calendar Count 2 (URG p. 16)

Kenji's birthday is on the ninth day of this month. Melissa's birthday is two weeks later. What is the date of Melissa's birthday?

J. Calendar Count 3 (URG p. 17)

Labor Day is on a Monday. Henrique's birthday is two weeks later.

1. On what day of the week is Henrique's birthday?
2. What is the date for Henrique's birthday?

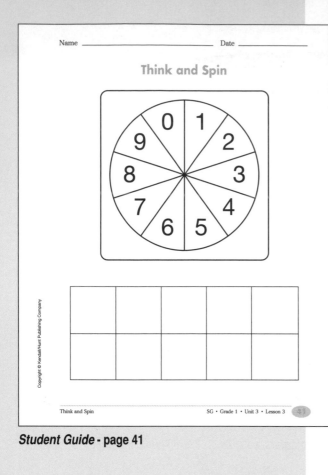

Student Guide - page 41

Use a clear spinner, the *Think and Spin* transparency, and the *Ten Frame Recording Sheet* transparency to introduce the activity on an overhead projector.

Spin the spinner. Record the number on a ten frame. Then, write a number sentence that fits the ten frame. For example, if a student spins a 6, he or she fills in six dots on the ten frame and may write sentences such as $6 + 4 = 10$ or $5 + 1 = 6$. The next spin should be recorded on a different ten frame. Encourage students to work in pairs to record and write number sentences.

Place this game on a games menu so students can play during free time. Label an envelope for game instructions and items and place in an accessible location.

Student Guide - page 43

Homework and Practice

- DPP items I and J use the calendar to develop and practice number sense skills.
- Send home the *Wearing Pockets* Homework Page so students will wear clothing with pockets for the data collection activity in Lesson 4.

Assessment

Use the *Observational Assessment Record* to note students' abilities to represent numbers using a ten frame and to write appropriate number sentences.

Name _____ Date _____

Wearing Pockets

Homework

Dear Family Member:

Tomorrow your child will gather data and make a bar graph. We will count the number of pockets on each student's clothing. Please help your child select clothing that has pockets on the pants, skirt, or shirt.

Thank you for your help.

Think and Spin   SG • Grade 1 • Unit 3 • Lesson 3   45

Student Guide - page 45

At a Glance

Math Facts Strategies and Daily Practice and Problems

DPP items I–J use the calendar to develop number sense.

Teaching the Activity (A2)

1. Introduce the activity with one student volunteer.
2. Student pairs need a pencil, a spinner, the *Think and Spin* Activity Page, and the *Ten Frame Recording Sheet*.
3. Students take turns spinning and writing number sentences.

Homework

Send home the *Wearing Pockets* Homework Page that asks students to wear clothing with pockets for the next math class.

Assessment

Use Assessment Indicator A2 and the *Observational Assessment Record* to document students' abilities to translate between representations of numbers (ten frames and symbols).

Notes:

Lesson 4

Pockets Graph

Lesson Overview

Using connecting cubes, students collect data by counting the pockets in their clothing. They then use this data to construct a group bar graph.

Key Content

- Collecting, organizing, graphing, and analyzing data.
- Using a bar graph to solve problems.
- Connecting mathematics to real-world situations.
- Translating between graphs and real-world events.

Key Vocabulary

- bar graph

Materials List

Supplies and Copies

Student	Teacher
Supplies for Each Student	**Supplies**
• 12 connecting cubes • self-adhesive note	• a group graph (see Before the Activity)
Copies	**Copies/Transparencies**

All blackline masters including assessment, transparency, and DPP masters are also on the Teacher Resource CD.

Daily Practice and Problems
DPP items K–N (*Unit Resource Guide* Pages 17–18)

Daily Practice and Problems

Suggestions for using the DPPs are on page 50.

K. How Many Shapes 1? (URG p. 17)

Place a blue rhombus and six green triangles on the overhead. How many blue rhombuses can you make with these triangles?

L. How Many Shapes 2? (URG p. 17)

Place a yellow hexagon and six blue rhombuses on the overhead. How many hexagons can you make with these blue rhombuses?

M. How Many Shapes 3? (URG p. 18)

Place a yellow hexagon and six red trapezoids on the overhead. How many hexagons can you make with these trapezoids?

N. What Do You Know About Triangles? (URG p. 18)

List all the things we know about triangles.

Before the Activity

Prepare a group graph on easel paper or on the board as shown in Figure 4. Make sure that your graph columns are large enough to hold the self-adhesive notes.

Allow adequate time to complete the data collection in one class session. The data won't be the same with a change of clothing.

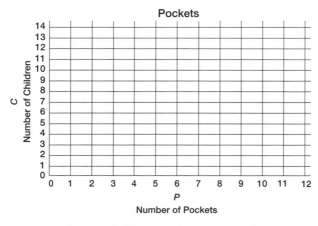

Figure 4: *The empty group graph*

Teaching the Activity

Instruct students to place one connecting cube in each pocket. Then tell students to take all the cubes out of their pockets and connect them to make a

cube train. Ask students to count the number of cubes in their trains.

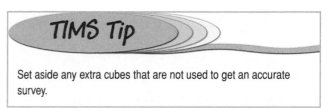

Set aside any extra cubes that are not used to get an accurate survey.

Ask all students with a given number of pockets (e.g., three pockets) to line up in front of the class and show their cube trains. Check that students have the right number of cubes in their trains by counting and comparing to see that all are the same length. Repeat this procedure with other numbers of pockets.

Instruct each student to write his or her name on a self-adhesive note. As you name a value from 0 to 12, students with that number of pockets (and length of cube train) bring their notes to the graph. Students should place their own self-adhesive notes on the graph to develop a concrete understanding of what a graph represents.

Make sure students place their notes on the lines above the numbers and not in the spaces between. This is a scientific convention that is used throughout the curriculum. A sample graph is shown in Figure 5 below.

Have a student who has no pockets place the self-adhesive note on the vertical axis—the zero line.

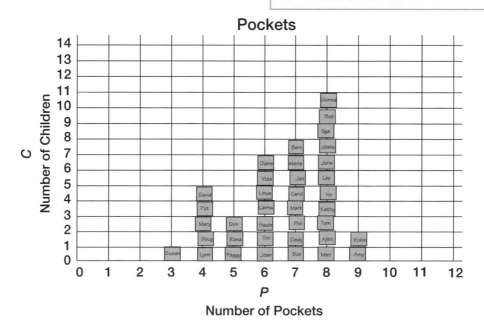

Figure 5: *Pockets Bar Graph*

Ask students with two pockets to stand. Count the number of students standing. Write the number on the board. Count the number of self-adhesive notes above the number two on the bar graph. Ask the following questions:

- *Should the number of students standing and the number of self-adhesive notes be the same? Why?*
- *If I read the names on the notes above the number two, should they be the names of the people standing? Why?*

Repeat this process with other numbers of pockets.

Begin the analysis of the data represented on the bar graph by asking students to think about what the graph is showing. Encourage them to ask questions about the data. This kind of discussion prompts students to reflect on the "story" the graph is telling.

If students do not think of the questions listed, introduce them into the discussion.

- *Which bar is tallest? What does that mean?*
- *Which bar is shortest? What does that mean?*
- *Who has the least number of pockets?*
- *Who has the most pockets?*
- *If a new student walked into the classroom, could we make a good estimate as to how many pockets he or she might have using the information from our graph?*
- *How many children have clothes with five pockets?*
- *How many children have clothes with four, five, or six pockets?*
- *Are students more likely to have six or seven pockets? Why?*

Students can use information directly from the graph or they can make predictions based on the data they collected.

Encourage students to explain how they found answers to each question. This will help students develop their mathematical communication skills.

Homework and Practice

DPP items K–N provide practice with geometry concepts.

Math Facts Strategies and Daily Practice and Problems

DPP items K–N review geometry concepts.

Teaching the Activity

1. Students place one connecting cube in each of their pockets.
2. Students remove the cubes from their pockets, count them, and make a train.
3. Ask students with a specific number of cubes or pockets to stand.
4. Check students' trains by counting and comparing their trains to others.
5. Students write their names on self-adhesive notes and place them on the graph.
6. Students ask and answer questions about the graph.

Notes:

Lesson 5

Pocket Parts

Lesson Overview

"Pockets on student clothing" is used as a context for exploring part-whole relationships of numbers. The techniques used here will serve as a bridge from the concrete (pockets) to the symbolic (numbers). Students gather data, record it, write number sentences, and discuss the part-whole relationships.

Key Content

- Translating between different representations of numbers.
- Collecting, organizing, and analyzing data.
- Communicating mathematics orally and in writing.
- Investigating the part-whole relationship of numbers.
- Connecting mathematics to real-world situations.
- Using the counting-on strategy to add.
- Developing and practicing math facts strategies.

Math Facts Strategies

Each activity in this lesson provides opportunities for students to develop and practice math fact strategies. DPP item V reviews counting on and counting back.

Homework

Use the *More Pocket Parts 1* and *More Pocket Parts 2* Blackline Masters to construct homework pages.

Assessment

1. Students complete the *Pockets* Assessment Page.
2. Use the *More Pocket Parts 1* or the *More Pocket Parts 2* Blackline Masters to develop a short assessment.
3. Use Assessment Indicators A3 and A6 and the *Observational Assessment Record* to document students' abilities to use manipulatives and the counting-on strategy to solve addition problems.

Curriculum Sequence

Before This Unit

In Kindergarten, students solved problems reflecting the problem types outlined in this lesson and in the Background. See Problem Solving in the Kindergarten Day in the Ongoing Content section of the Kindergarten *Teacher Resource Book.*

After This Unit

Students continue to work on different problem types for the remainder of first grade. For more information see the Background for Units 4, 6, 13, and 14 and the TIMS Tutor: *Word Problems* in the *Teacher Implementation Guide.*

Materials List

Supplies and Copies

Student	Teacher
Supplies for Each Student Pair • 30 connecting cubes (10 cubes in 3 colors)	**Supplies** • easel paper, optional
Copies • copies* of *More Pocket Parts 1* for extra problems (*Unit Resource Guide* Page 62) • copies* of *More Pocket Parts 2* for extra problems (*Unit Resource Guide* Page 63) *fill in numbers to create problems before copying	**Copies/Transparencies** • 1 transparency of *Five-column Data Table* (*Unit Resource Guide* Page 64) or easel paper for a five-column data table • 1 transparency of *Shirt, Pants, and Coat Pockets* (*Unit Resource Guide* Page 61) • 1 transparency of *Hidden Pockets* (*Student Guide* Page 52)

All blackline masters including assessment, transparency, and DPP masters are also on the Teacher Resource CD.

Student Books
Shirt and Pants Pockets (*Student Guide* Page 47)
Pocket Parts 1 (*Student Guide* Page 49)
Pocket Parts 2 (*Student Guide* Page 50)
How Many Pockets? (*Student Guide* Page 51)
Hidden Pockets (*Student Guide* Page 52)
Pockets (*Student Guide* Page 53)

Daily Practice and Problems
DPP items O–V (*Unit Resource Guide* Pages 18–20)

Assessment Tools
Observational Assessment Record (*Unit Resource Guide* Pages 11–12)

Daily Practice and Problems

Suggestions for using the DPPs are on page 59.

O. What Do You Know About Squares?
(URG p. 18)

List all the things we know about squares.

P. Calendar Count 4 (URG p. 18)

1. Today is ___. (Date)
   In eleven days it will be ___.
2. Today is ___. (Day)
   In eleven days it will be ___.

Q. Calendar Count 5 (URG p. 19)

1. What are the names of the months?
2. How many months are in one year?

R. Calendar Count 6 (URG p. 19)

1. What is the first month of the year?
2. What is the last month of the year?

S. Calendar Count 7 (URG p. 19)

1. In which month is your birthday?
2. Find another student who was born in the same month as you.

T. What Do You Know About Rhombuses? (URG p. 19)

List all the things we know about rhombuses.

U. What Do You Know About Hexagons? (URG p. 19)

List all the things we know about hexagons.

V. What Number Once Again?
(URG p. 20)

1. What number follows ten?
2. What number comes just before ten?
3. What number follows twelve?
4. What number comes just before twelve?

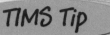

TIMS Tip

The Background for this unit and the Tims Tutor: *Word Problems* provide information on addition problem types. Both documents emphasize the importance of children using strategies that make sense to them.

Before the Activity

Create a five-column data table on easel paper, the chalkboard, or on a transparency. See Figure 6 for column headings.

The *More Pocket Parts 1* and *More Pocket Parts 2* Blackline Masters allow you to fill in the numbers according to your students' needs. You may want to prepare several versions of these pages ahead of time so they are available for additional practice, homework assignments, or assessment.

Teaching the Activity

Part 1 Combining Two Parts and Finding the Whole

Ask students to make a cube train using one color for the number of their shirt pockets and another cube train using a second color for the number of their pants pockets. Have students join the two trains. This represents the total number of pockets.

Name _____ Date _____

Shirt and Pants Pockets

Record the number of shirt pockets, pants pockets, and total pockets. Then, write a number sentence.

☐ + ☐ = ☐

Copyright © Kendall/Hunt Publishing Company

Pocket Parts   SG • Grade 1 • Unit 3 • Lesson 5   47

Student Guide - page 47 *(Answers on p. 65)*

Content Note

Research from the Cognitively Guided Instruction (CGI) Project provides interesting observations about children's approaches to problem solving. The researchers observe that there is a great deal of commonality in the strategies that children use to solve word problems. A child typically moves through these three stages: modeling, counting, and using derived number facts. Children move back and forth through the strategies depending on the size of the numbers. At the same time, there is a great deal of variability in the ages at which children use different strategies. (Carpenter, et al., 1999)

Observe students as they work in pairs to complete the tasks in this lesson. Encourage them to explain or model how they solved the problems so that you can understand the different strategies individual students use.

Ask students to turn to the *Shirt and Pants Pockets* Activity Page and record the number of shirt and pants pockets according to their clothes and their trains. Ask each student to write a number sentence representing the number of pockets on his or her clothing. As an example, write a number sentence for the number of pockets on your clothing.

Ask several students to explain to the class how many shirt pockets, pants pockets, and total pockets they have. Also ask them to share their number sentences.

TIMS Tip

Students may write the number of shirt pockets first in their number sentences. If a child reverses the order of the parts, take the opportunity to point out that the whole is not affected. For example, 3 shirt pockets + 2 pants pockets = 5 pockets is the same as 2 pants pockets + 3 shirt pockets = 5 pockets.

Choose a total number of pockets to study, such as five. Ask the children who have a total of five pockets to stand and show the class their pictures. Each student should explain how many shirt pockets, pants pockets, and total pockets he or she has. Record this information on the data table. Complete the table showing the different combinations that make five. See the examples in Figure 6.

Pocket Parts				
Name	Shirt Pockets	Pants Pockets	Total Pockets	Number Sentence
Brandon	1	4	5	1 + 4 = 5
Nila	0	5	5	0 + 5 = 5
Linda	2	3	5	2 + 3 = 5

Figure 6: *Pocket Parts Data Table*

Students practice finding the total number of pockets and writing number sentences on the *Pocket Parts 1* and *Pocket Parts 2* Activity Pages. Students may complete these individually or with a partner. Encourage students to use counters or to make tallies on the pictures of each piece of clothing and then count the tallies.

For additional practice, write your own version using the *More Pocket Parts 1* Blackline Master.

Student Guide - page 49 (Answers on p. 65)

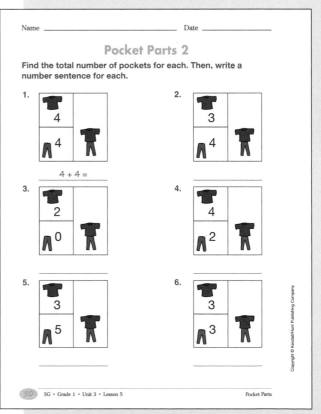

Student Guide - page 50 (Answers on p. 66)

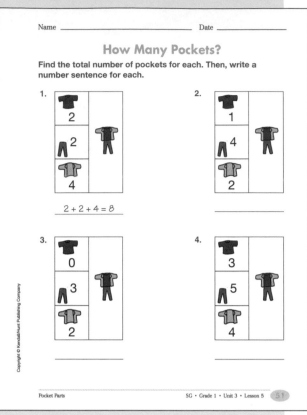

Student Guide - page 51 (Answers on p. 66)

Student Guide - page 52 (Answers on p. 67)

Part 2 Combining Three Parts and Finding the Whole

Students find the total number of pockets by adding the shirt, pants, and coat pockets. Use the *Shirt, Pants, and Coat Pockets* Transparency Master to create a problem for the class. Build three, different-colored towers to represent the number of pockets in each piece of clothing. Attach the three towers and count the total number of cubes. Encourage students to use the counting-on strategy when appropriate rather than counting from one. Write a number sentence. After students build towers and write number sentences for several problems, ask them to complete the *How Many Pockets?* Activity Page.

> ### TIMS Tip
>
> Not every student will need counters, but have them readily available for those who choose to use them.

Part 3 Finding the Missing Part

Before the children begin work on the *Hidden Pockets* Activity Page, guide the class in thinking about how they can solve these problems. Use the following prompts and a few students as examples:

- *Becky is wearing clothes with pockets today. She counted all her pockets and has six altogether. We can see four pockets on her shirt, but we cannot see the pockets on her pants. What do we know in this problem?* (The number of pockets on Becky's shirt and the total number of pockets.)

- *How can we find the number of hidden pockets on her pants? Who has an idea about how to find out?*

Offer additional prompts as needed to help children talk about what is known and what they need to find out. It is important that children do the thinking and learn to explain their ideas to the rest of the class. If children do not offer strategies, encourage students to work in pairs to develop more ideas. Repeat the above process using a few more children in the classroom.

Ask children to work with a partner to solve the problems on the *Hidden Pockets* Activity Page. Two strategies that children may use to solve these problems are listed next and shown in Figure 7.

- Place counters on the total number of pockets. Slide the number of counters that represent the shirt pockets to the shirt, slide the remaining counters to the pants, and then record the number of counters representing the pants pockets.
- Build cube towers to show the two known numbers and count up to find the difference between the number of cubes in each tower. This strategy was used in DPP items in Unit 2.

Figure 7: *Two possible strategies for solving* Hidden Pockets *problems*

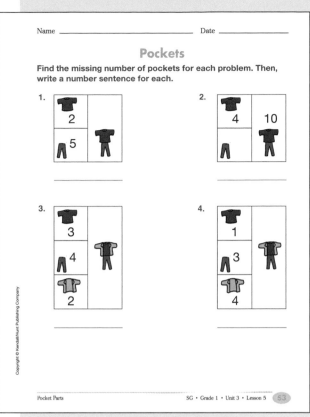
Student Guide - page 53 (Answers on p. 67)

Math Facts Strategies

- Each activity in this lesson provides opportunities for students to develop and practice math facts strategies.
- DPP item V reviews counting on and counting back.

Homework and Practice

- Use the *More Pocket Parts 1* and *More Pocket Parts 2* Blackline Masters to write homework activities.
- DPP items O and T–U review geometry.
- DPP items P–S focus on time as measured on the calendar.

Assessment

- Use the *Pockets* Assessment Page.
- Use the *More Pocket Parts 1* or *More Pocket Parts 2* Blackline Masters to write an assessment.
- Use the *Observational Assessment Record* to note students' abilities to use the counting-on strategy to add and to use manipulatives to solve addition problems.

At a Glance

Math Facts Strategies and Daily Practice and Problems

DPP items O and T–U review geometry. DPP item V reviews counting on and counting back. DPP items P–S focus on the calendar.

Part 1. Combining Two Parts and Finding the Whole (A1) (A3) (A6)

1. Students use connecting cubes to find the total number of their pockets. They record the number of pockets and a number sentence on the *Shirt and Pants Pockets* Activity Page.
2. Students share their work and number sentences.
3. Choose a total number of pockets to study, such as seven. Complete a table showing the different combinations that make seven.
4. Students complete *Pocket Parts 1* and *Pocket Parts 2* Activity Pages.

Part 2. Combining Three Parts and Finding the Whole (A2) (A3)

1. Using the *Shirt, Pants, and Coat Pockets* Transparency Master, present a problem giving the number of shirt, pants, and coat pockets.
2. Students use cubes to find the total number of pockets and record number sentences.
3. Students complete the *How Many Pockets?* Activity Page.

Part 3. Finding the Missing Part (A2) (A3)

1. Present a problem in which the number of shirt pockets and the total number of pockets are known, but the number of pants pockets is missing.
2. Ask students questions leading to possible ways to solve the problems.
3. Students record a number sentence.
4. Students complete the *Hidden Pockets* Activity Page.

Homework

Use the *More Pocket Parts 1* and *More Pocket Parts 2* Blackline Masters to construct homework pages.

Assessment

1. Students complete the *Pockets* Assessment Page.
2. Use the *More Pocket Parts 1* or the *More Pocket Parts 2* Blackline Masters to develop a short assessment.
3. Use Assessment Indicators A3 and A6 and the *Observational Assessment Record* to document students' abilities to use manipulatives and the counting-on strategy to solve addition problems.

Answer Key is on pages 65–67.

Notes:

Shirt, Pants, and Coat Pockets

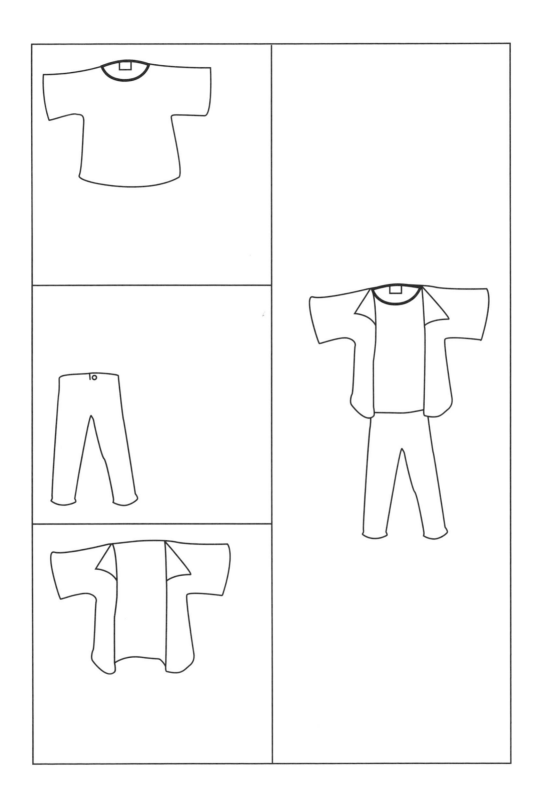

More Pocket Parts 1

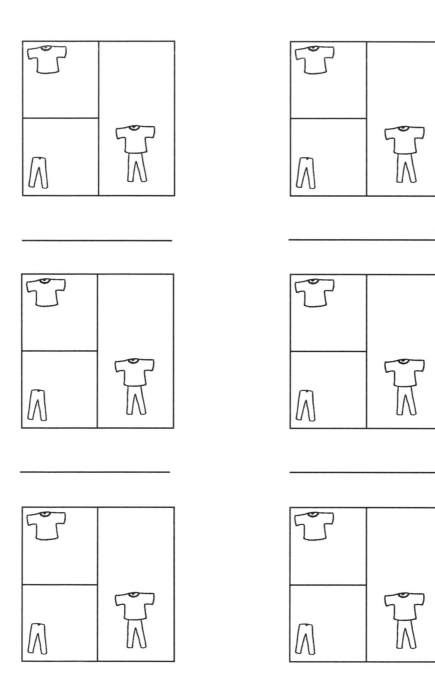

More Pocket Parts 2

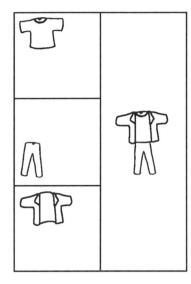

_____

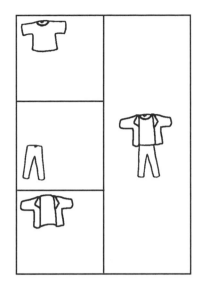

_____

_____

_____

Name _____ Date _____

_____

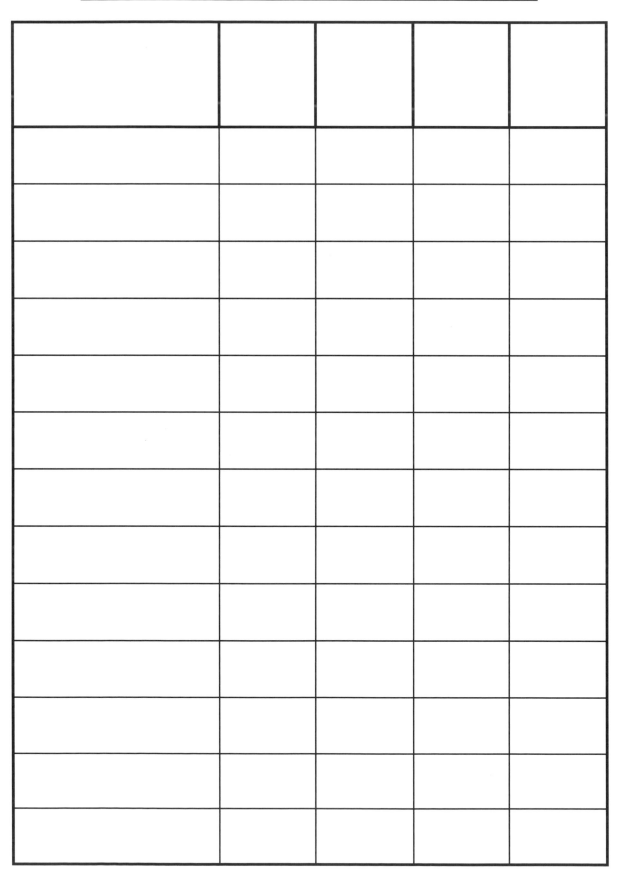

Five-column Data Table, Blackline Master

Student Guide (p. 47)

Shirt and Pants Pockets

Answers will vary.*

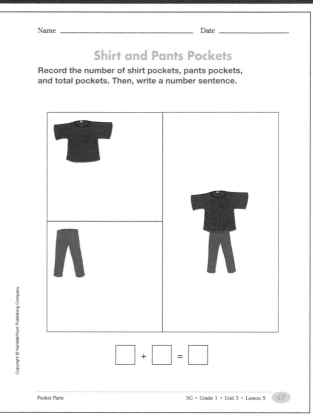

Student Guide - page 47

Student Guide (p. 49)

Pocket Parts 1

1. $1 + 4 = 5$
2. $2 + 3 = 5$
3. $1 + 2 = 3$
4. $2 + 5 = 7$
5. $1 + 3 = 4$
6. $0 + 3 = 3$

Student Guide - page 49

*Answers and/or discussion are included in the Lesson Guide.

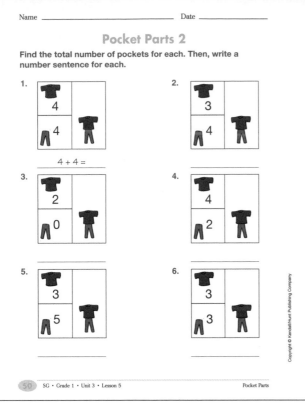

Student Guide (p. 50)

Pocket Parts 2

1. $4 + 4 = 8$
2. $3 + 4 = 7$
3. $2 + 0 = 2$
4. $4 + 2 = 6$
5. $3 + 5 = 8$
6. $3 + 3 = 6$

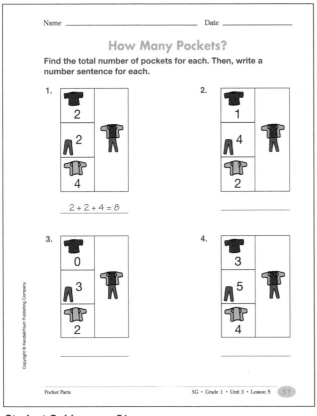

Student Guide (p. 51)

How Many Pockets?

1. $2 + 2 + 4 = 8$
2. $1 + 4 + 2 = 7$
3. $0 + 3 + 2 = 5$
4. $3 + 5 + 4 = 12$

Student Guide (p. 52)

Hidden Pockets

I. $2 + 3 = 5$

2. Fay's pockets: $3 + 4 = 7$

3. Kay's pockets: $0 + 2 = 2$

4. Ray's pockets: $1 + 5 = 6$

5. May's pockets: $2 + 2 = 4$

6. Shay's pockets: $4 + 5 = 9$

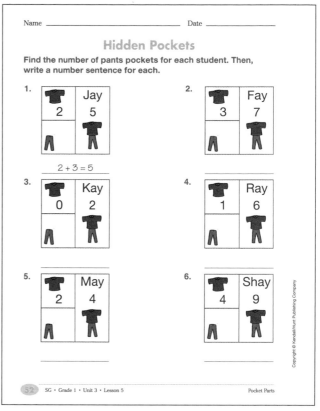

Student Guide - page 52

Student Guide (p. 53)

Pockets

I. $2 + 5 = 7$

2. $4 + 6 = 10$

3. $3 + 4 + 2 = 9$

4. $1 + 3 + 4 = 8$

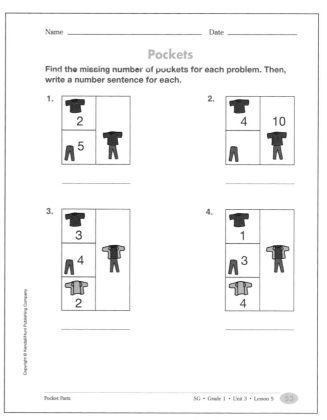

Student Guide - page 53

Lesson 6

What's in That Pocket?

Lesson Overview

Estimated Class Sessions

3

Students partition the number ten into two and three parts. They practice writing number sentences and finding missing parts.

Key Content

- Translating between different representations of a number.
- Partitioning a number into two and three parts.
- Writing addition number sentences.
- Organizing and analyzing data in a table.
- Solving addition problems and explaining strategies.
- Using manipulatives to solve problems.

Math Facts Strategies

DPP items X, Y, AA, and BB review addition facts strategies. DPP item W reviews counting patterns necessary for counting on and counting back.

Homework

Assign the *Eight Pennies Data Table* Homework Page.

Assessment

1. Students complete the *Nine Pennies Data Table* Assessment Page.
2. Use DPP item Y as an assessment.
3. Use Assessment Indicators A2 and A4 and the *Observational Assessment Record* to document students' abilities to partition numbers and translate their work into addition number sentences.

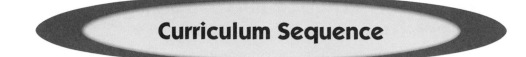

Curriculum Sequence

Before This Unit

Students regularly partitioned numbers in Kindergarten with particular emphasis on the numbers 5 and 10. See lessons in the Number Sense Strand in Months 3, 4, 7, and 8.

After This Unit

Students will continue to partition numbers throughout first grade as a way to develop math facts strategies. Students partition numbers 0–100 in Units 5, 8, 11, and 13.

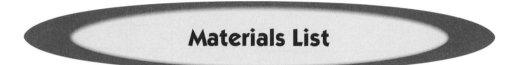

Materials List

Supplies and Copies

Student	Teacher
Supplies for Each Student • 10 pennies	**Supplies** • 10 pennies • blank transparency
Copies • 1 copy of *Ten Frames* per student (*Unit Resource Guide* Page 76)	**Copies/Transparencies**

All blackline masters including assessment, transparency, and DPP masters are also on the Teacher Resource CD.

Student Books

Two Pockets Work Mat (*Student Guide* Page 55)
Two Pockets Data Table (*Student Guide* Page 57)
Three Pockets Work Mat (*Student Guide* Page 58)
Three Pockets Data Table (*Student Guide* Page 59)
Eight Pennies Data Table (*Student Guide* Page 61)
Nine Pennies Data Table (*Student Guide* Page 63)

Daily Practice and Problems

DPP items W–BB (*Unit Resource Guide* Pages 20–22)

Assessment Tools

Observational Assessment Record (*Unit Resource Guide* Pages 11–12)

Daily Practice and Problems

Suggestions for using the DPPs are on pages 73–74.

W. What Number Once More?

(URG p. 20)

1. What number follows fifteen?
2. What number comes just before fifteen?
3. What number follows nineteen?
4. What number comes just before nineteen?

X. Penny Problems 1 (URG p. 20)

You have ten pennies. Three pennies are in your shirt pocket. The rest are in your pants pocket. How many pennies are in your pants pocket?

Y. Penny Problems 2 (URG p. 21)

1. Sue found ten pennies in her pockets. Eight pennies were in her shirt pocket. How many were in her pants pocket?
2. Sue found eight pennies in her pockets. One penny was in a shirt pocket. Four pennies were in her pants pockets. How many were in her coat pocket?

Z. Tallies (URG p. 21)

T.J. has a shell collection. He listed all the colors of his shells: white, gray, white, tan, gray, gray, pink, gray, tan, pink, pink, gray, white, and gray. Use tallies to record the colors of T.J.'s shells in the table below.

Color	Tallies	Number
Pink		
Gray		
White		
Tan		

Then, write the number of shells for each color.

AA. Pennies (URG p. 22)

Emily has 6 pennies. Complete the table below to show different ways Emily can place her 6 pennies into 2 pockets. Then, write a number sentence for each.

Pocket 1	Pocket 2	Number Sentence
0¢	6¢	0¢ + 6¢ = 6¢

BB. More Pennies (URG p. 22)

Tyler has 5 pennies. Complete the table below to show different ways Tyler can place his 5 pennies into 3 pockets. Then, write a number sentence for each.

Pocket 1	Pocket 2	Pocket 3	Number Sentence
1¢	1¢	3¢	1¢ + 1¢ + 3¢ = 5¢

Make a four-column and a five-column data table on the chalkboard, similar to the tables on the *Two Pockets Data Table* and the *Three Pockets Data Table* Activity Pages in the *Student Guide*.

Teaching the Activity

Part 1 Partitioning Ten into Two Parts

The *Two Pockets Work Mat* in the *Student Guide* has a picture of a red and a blue pocket. Using a red and blue transparency marker, draw two pockets on a transparency. Make the pockets large enough to fit ten pennies.

Tell students they are going to put their ten pennies into two pockets using their *Two Pockets Work Mat*. Place six pennies in the red pocket and four pennies in the blue pocket as an example. Ask:

- *How many pennies are in the red pocket?* (6)
- *How many pennies are in the blue pocket?* (4)
- *What number sentence can I write to describe my pennies?* (6 + 4 = 10)
- *Is this the only way I can divide the ten pennies in my two pockets?*

Encourage students to show other ways to divide the pennies. Since there is more than one way to solve this problem, tell them they will keep track of all the different ways in a data table. Have students record the data, including the number sentence, on the *Two Pockets Data Table* Activity Page.

Ask students to come to the overhead and share their solutions. After each child places the pennies in the pockets, ask the class if this is a different solution. Encourage students to refer to the data table. If the solution does not already exist, record it. Students should also record each solution at their desks to practice filling in a data table.

Solutions where the pennies are reversed in the two pockets (e.g., four pennies in the blue and six in the red when a previous entry had six pennies in the blue and four in the red) are two different solutions. Ask:

- *What happens to the total number of pennies when the numbers on the data table are turned around?* (The total is the same.)

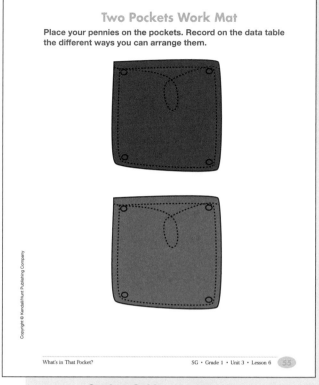

Student Guide - page 55 (Answers on p. 77)

Two Pockets Data Table

How many ways can you arrange ten pennies in two pockets? Record as many ways as you can. Then, write a number sentence for each one.

		Total Pennies	Number Sentence
6	4	10	6 + 4 = 10

Student Guide - page 57 (Answers on p. 77)

After students share their solutions, you might present a challenge:

- *Do we have all the possible ways to arrange the ten pennies into two pockets?*
- *How can we find out if we have all the possible answers?*

Encourage the class to work together to find all the possible answers. There are eleven possible solutions as shown in Figure 8. Ask pairs to report their solutions as you record them on the class data table. Reorganize the data table so the numbers in each column go in order. Ask:

- *What patterns do you see in the data table?* (Answers will vary. Students may notice that organizing the data will help show any missing answers. Students may notice that if the numbers in the first column decrease by one, the numbers in the second column increase by one.)

TIMS Tip

Remind students that putting zero pennies in the red pocket or zero pennies in the blue pocket is a possibility.

		Total Pennies	Number Sentence
10	0	10	$10 + 0 = 10$
9	1	10	$9 + 1 = 10$
8	2	10	$8 + 2 = 10$
7	3	10	$7 + 3 = 10$
6	4	10	$6 + 4 = 10$
5	5	10	$5 + 5 = 10$
4	6	10	$4 + 6 = 10$
3	7	10	$3 + 7 = 10$
2	8	10	$2 + 8 = 10$
1	9	10	$1 + 9 = 10$
0	10	10	$0 + 10 = 10$

Figure 8: *Data table with eleven possible answers*

Part 2 Partitioning Ten into Three Parts

This activity is similar to the previous one, except that children will use the *Three Pockets Work Mat* and the *Three Pockets Data Table*. Students find different ways to arrange ten pennies into three pockets. There are 66 ways of arranging the pennies if you allow one or two pockets to have no pennies. There are 36 possibilities if each pocket has at least one penny. Children should realize they are finding just a few of the possible answers. Encourage students to write number sentences with three parts and a total.

Math Facts Strategies

DPP items X, Y, AA, and BB review addition facts strategies in the context of money in pockets. DPP item W reviews counting patterns necessary for counting on and counting back.

Homework and Practice

- Assign the *Eight Pennies Data Table* Homework Page. Families will help their children find different ways to arrange eight pennies into two pockets. Students record the data in the table and write a number sentence for each arrangement.

- DPP item Z practices using tallies.

Name _____ Date _____

Three Pockets Work Mat

Place your pennies on the pockets. Record on the data table different ways you can arrange them.

58 SG • Grade 1 • Unit 3 • Lesson 6   What's in That Pocket?

Student Guide - page 58 (Answers on p. 78)

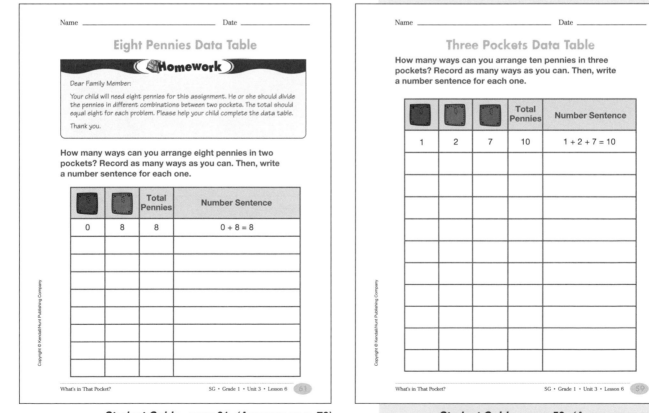

Name _____ Date _____

Eight Pennies Data Table

Homework

Dear Family Member:

Your child will need eight pennies for this assignment. He or she should divide the pennies in different combinations between two pockets. The total should equal eight for each problem. Please help your child complete the data table.

Thank you.

How many ways can you arrange eight pennies in two pockets? Record as many ways as you can. Then, write a number sentence for each one.

		Total Pennies	Number Sentence
0	8	8	0 + 8 = 8

What's in That Pocket?   SG • Grade 1 • Unit 3 • Lesson 6 61

Student Guide - page 61 (Answers on p. 79)

Name _____ Date _____

Three Pockets Data Table

How many ways can you arrange ten pennies in three pockets? Record as many ways as you can. Then, write a number sentence for each one.

			Total Pennies	Number Sentence
1	2	7	10	1 + 2 + 7 = 10

What's in That Pocket?   SG • Grade 1 • Unit 3 • Lesson 6 59

Student Guide - page 59 (Answers on p. 78)

Name _____ Date _____

Nine Pennies Data Table

How many ways can you arrange nine pennies in two pockets? Record as many ways as you can. Then, write a number sentence for each one.

		Total Pennies	Number Sentence

What's in That Pocket?   SG • Grade 1 • Unit 3 • Lesson 6   63

Student Guide - page 63 *(Answers on p. 79)*

Assessment

- Students complete the *Nine Pennies Data Table* Assessment Page. Students must find different ways to place nine pennies into two pockets. Assess whether students can partition nine into two parts in more than one way and whether they can write a corresponding number sentence. Encourage children to find as many ways as they can, but don't expect them to find all the ways.

- Use DPP item Y as a performance assessment. Give students pennies and a copy of *Ten Frames* to solve the problem.

- Record your observations on the *Observational Assessment Record,* noting students' progress in partitioning numbers and using symbols to write corresponding number sentences.

Extension

When students present their solutions at the overhead projector, ask them to place pennies only in the red pocket. The rest of the class must decide how many pennies should go in the blue pocket, so that the total is ten. This is similar to Part 2 of Lesson 5.

At a Glance

Math Facts Strategies and Daily Practice and Problems

DPP items X, Y, AA, and BB review addition facts strategies. DPP item W reviews number patterns. DPP item Z practices using tallies.

Part 1. Partitioning Ten into Two Parts (A2) (A4)

1. Draw a picture of a red pocket and a blue pocket on a transparency.
2. Make one four-column data table and one five-column data table on the chalkboard.
3. Tell students they are going to put ten pennies into two pockets using the *Two Pockets Work Mat* in the *Student Guide.*
4. Place six pennies in the red pocket and four pennies in the blue pocket. Write a number sentence $(6 + 4 = 10)$.
5. Encourage students to show other ways to divide the pennies and write number sentences.
6. Students record their solutions in the *Two Pockets Data Table.*
7. Reorganize the data table so numbers in the blue pocket go in order from 0 to 10. Ask students to describe patterns they see.

Part 2. Partitioning Ten into Three Parts (A2) (A4)

1. Draw a picture of a red pocket, a blue pocket, and a green pocket on a transparency.
2. Tell students they are going to put ten pennies into three pockets using the *Three Pockets Work Mat.*
3. Students record possible arrangements and write number sentences in the *Three Pockets Data Table.*

Homework

Assign the *Eight Pennies Data Table* Homework Page.

Assessment

1. Students complete the *Nine Pennies Data Table* Assessment Page.
2. Use DPP item Y as an assessment.
3. Use Assessment Indicators A2 and A4 and the *Observational Assessment Record* to document students' abilities to partition numbers and translate their work into addition number sentences.

Extension

Have a student at the overhead place pennies only on the red pocket. The class can decide how many pennies should go in the blue pocket so that the total is ten.

Answer Key is on pages 77–79.

Notes:

Ten Frames

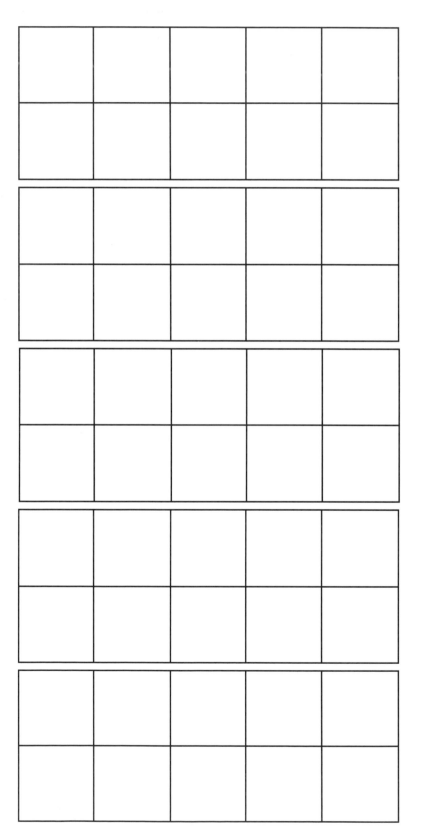

Blackline Master

Student Guide (p. 55)

Two Pockets Work Mat

Students' work will vary.

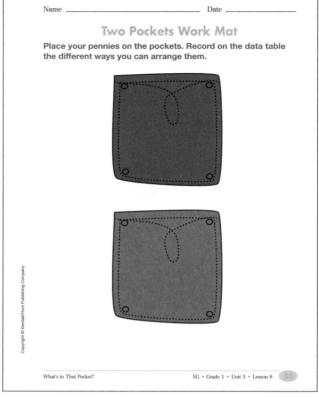

Student Guide - page 55

Student Guide (p. 57)

Two Pockets Data Table

See Figure 8 in Lesson Guide 6.*

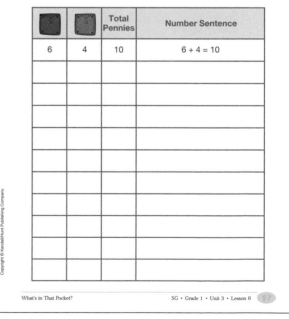

Student Guide - page 57

*Answers and/or discussion are included in the Lesson Guide.

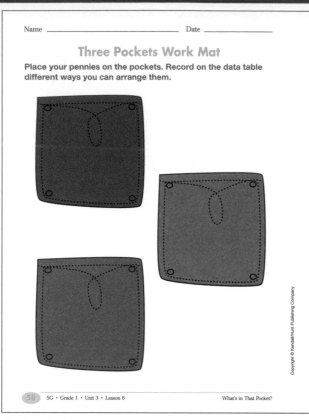

Student Guide - page 58

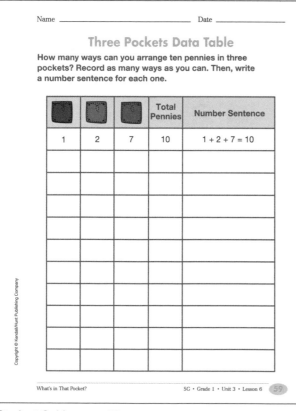

Student Guide - page 59

Student Guide (p. 58)

Three Pockets Work Mat

Students' work will vary.

Student Guide (p. 59)

Three Pockets Data Table

Students' solutions will vary. There are 66 possible number sentences. There are 36 possible sentences if every pocket has at least one penny. Some sample sentences are shown in the following table.

✉	✉	✉	Total Pennies	Number Sentence
0	0	10	10	0 + 0 + 10 = 10
1	0	9	10	1 + 0 + 9 = 10
2	1	7	10	2 + 1 + 7 = 10
3	0	7	10	3 + 0 + 7 = 10
4	2	4	10	4 + 2 + 4 = 10
5	5	0	10	5 + 5 + 0 = 10
6	0	4	10	6 + 0 + 4 = 10
6	2	2	10	6 + 2 + 2 = 10
8	1	1	10	8 + 1 + 1 = 10
5	3	2	10	5 + 3 + 2 = 10
4	3	3	10	4 + 3 + 3 = 10

Student Guide (p. 61)

Eight Pennies Data Table

🖐	🖐	Total Pennies	Number Sentence
0	8	8	$0 + 8 = 8$
1	7	8	$1 + 7 = 8$
2	6	8	$2 + 6 = 8$
3	5	8	$3 + 5 = 8$
4	4	8	$4 + 4 = 8$
5	3	8	$5 + 3 = 8$
6	2	8	$6 + 2 = 8$
7	1	8	$7 + 1 = 8$
8	0	8	$8 + 0 = 8$

Name _____ Date _____

Eight Pennies Data Table

Homework

Dear Family Member:

Your child will need eight pennies for this assignment. He or she should divide the pennies in different combinations between two pockets. The total should equal eight for each problem. Please help your child complete the data table.

Thank you.

How many ways can you arrange eight pennies in two pockets? Record as many ways as you can. Then, write a number sentence for each one.

		Total Pennies	Number Sentence
0	8	8	$0 + 8 = 8$

What's in That Pocket? SG • Grade 1 • Unit 3 • Lesson 6 61

Student Guide - page 61

Student Guide (p. 63)

Nine Pennies Data Table

🖐	🖐	Total Pennies	Number Sentence
0	9	9	$0 + 9 = 9$
1	8	9	$1 + 8 = 9$
2	7	9	$2 + 7 = 9$
3	6	9	$3 + 6 = 9$
4	5	9	$4 + 5 = 9$
5	4	9	$5 + 4 = 9$
6	3	9	$6 + 3 = 9$
7	2	9	$7 + 2 = 9$
8	1	9	$8 + 1 = 9$
9	0	9	$9 + 0 = 9$

Name _____ Date _____

Nine Pennies Data Table

How many ways can you arrange nine pennies in two pockets? Record as many ways as you can. Then, write a number sentence for each one.

		Total Pennies	Number Sentence

What's in That Pocket? SG • Grade 1 • Unit 3 • Lesson 6 63

Student Guide - page 63

Lesson 7

Purchasing with Pennies

Lesson Overview

Students solve problems as they use pennies and price tags to "purchase" items in a classroom store. They explore multiple strategies for finding solutions.

Key Content

- Solving word problems in several ways.
- Explaining, comparing, and contrasting solution methods.

Math Facts Strategies

DPP items CC and DD practice addition math facts strategies within the context of money in pockets.

Homework

Students complete the *What Would I Buy?* Homework Page.

Assessment

1. Use Assessment Indicators A3, A5, and A6 and the *Observational Assessment Record* to document students' abilities to solve addition problems using different strategies and to explain their reasoning.
2. Transfer appropriate documentation from the *Observational Assessment Record* to students' *Individual Assessement Record Sheets*.

Materials List

Supplies and Copies

Student	Teacher
Supplies for Each Student • 10 pennies or other counters	**Supplies**
Copies • 1 copy of *Ten Frames* per student, optional (*Unit Resource Guide* Page 76)	**Copies/Transparencies**

All blackline masters including assessment, transparency, and DPP masters are also on the Teacher Resource CD.

Student Books
Ten Frames (*Student Guide* Page 35)
What Would I Buy? (*Student Guide* Page 65)

Daily Practice and Problems
Daily items CC–DD (*Unit Resource Guide* Page 23)

Assessment Tools
Observational Assessment Record (*Unit Resource Guide* Pages 11–12)
Individual Assessment Record Sheet (*Teacher Implementation Guide,* Assessment section)

Daily Practice and Problems

Suggestions for using the DPPs are on page 83.

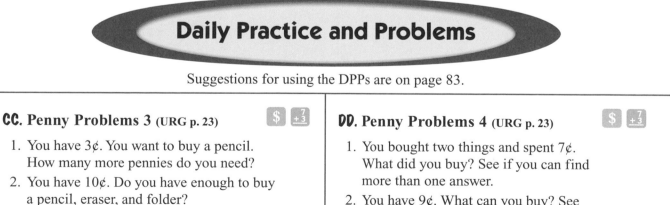

CC. Penny Problems 3 (URG p. 23)

1. You have 3¢. You want to buy a pencil. How many more pennies do you need?
2. You have 10¢. Do you have enough to buy a pencil, eraser, and folder?

DD. Penny Problems 4 (URG p. 23)

1. You bought two things and spent 7¢. What did you buy? See if you can find more than one answer.
2. You have 9¢. What can you buy? See if you can find more than one answer.

Students may contribute items from their desk for the display.

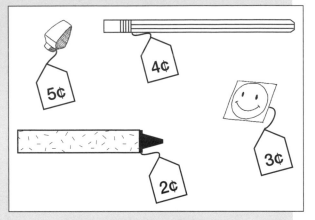

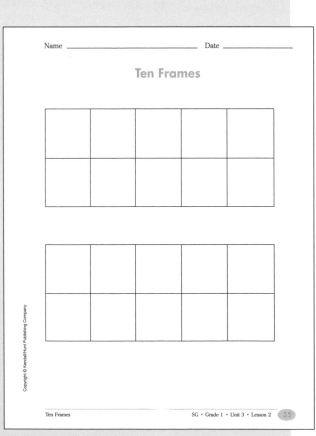

Figure 9: *Items with price tags*

Before the Activity

Bring in four objects and create price tags. The objects can be thematically related, such as items found in a toy store. Other good ideas include "selling" classroom items such as a sticker, pencil, crayon, and eraser.

Content Note

Four basic types of problems will be used in this activity:
1. Join — Result Unknown
   Leticia wants to buy a sticker and a pencil. How many pennies does she need?
2. Separate
   Carlos has 7¢. He wants to buy a pencil. How much money will he have left?
3. Comparison
   How much more is an eraser than a pencil?
4. Join — Change Unknown
   Phyllis has 3¢. She wants to buy an eraser. How many pennies should she borrow from a friend?

See the Background for this unit and the Tims Tutor: *Word Problems* for more information.

Teaching the Activity

This activity involves solving problems using items in a classroom store. First, discuss the "¢" sign. Show a penny, and indicate that we call it "one cent." We write "¢" instead of "cent" because it is shorter.

Distribute ten pennies to each student. Pose a problem such as a "join" problem. Ask children to use their pennies and the *Ten Frame* Activity Page to work through the problem. For example, to solve "How much would I have to pay if I buy a crayon and a pencil?" students place two pennies on the ten frame and then four pennies. Observe students to see the various ways they go about finding answers. When the groups finish working, have some children share their ways of finding the answer.

TIMS Tip

Use copies of the *Ten Frames* page from Lesson 6, if students no longer have a clean copy of the *Ten Frames* Activity Page.

Give the class more problems to solve, perhaps trying different types of problems. You might also have children create their own problems. An important part of this work is letting children share how they go about solving problems. Here are some sample problems:

- *You have 10¢. Can you buy a pencil and an eraser? How much money will you have left over?*

- *You bought two things and spent 7¢. What did you buy? See if you can find more than one answer.*

- *You have 9¢. How many crayons can you buy? How many erasers? pencils? stickers?*

- *You have 10¢. If you buy two crayons and one eraser, how much money will you have left over?*

- *You have 9¢. You want to buy a pencil and a sticker. Can you buy anything else?*

Students will solve similar problems throughout the year in the Daily Practice and Problems.

Math Facts Strategies

DPP items CC and DD practice addition math facts strategies within the context of money in pockets.

Homework and Practice

Students complete the *What Would I Buy?* Homework Page.

Assessment

- Use the *Observational Assessment Record* to note students' progress in solving addition problems using the counting-on strategy, manipulatives, or other strategies. Note also their abilities to explain their reasoning.

- Transfer appropriate assessment documentation from the Unit 3 *Observational Assessment Record* to students' *Individual Assessment Record Sheets.*

Name _____ Date _____

What Would I Buy?

Homework

Dear Family Member:
Look at the items below with your child. Ask him or her to read the price for each item. Help your child with the reading of each question. Give your child pennies to help him or her decide which items to circle. To answer Question 2, your child could draw a picture or use a number sentence (for example, 5¢ + 3¢ = 8¢).

Thank you for your cooperation.

Look at the items below.

5¢   4¢   3¢   2¢

1. Circle the items you would buy if you had ten pennies. (If you want two of the same item, make two circles around it.)

2. How much would you pay for all the items you circled? Show how you found your answer.

   _____

3. Would you have any pennies left over? How many?

   _____

4. Make up a problem for other students to solve.

   _____

Purchasing with Pennies

SG • Grade 1 • Unit 3 • Lesson 7   65

Student Guide* - page 65 *(Answers on p. 85)

URG • Grade 1 • Unit 3 • Lesson 7   83

At a Glance

Math Facts Strategies and Daily Practice and Problems

DPP items CC and DD practice addition math facts strategies using the context of money in pockets.

Teaching the Activity (A3) (A5) (A6)

1. Display four objects with price tags.
2. Introduce the "¢" sign.
3. Distribute pennies and empty ten frames to students.
4. Pose a "join" problem involving the four items.
5. Pose additional problems using the discussion prompts in the Lesson Guide.

Homework

Students complete the *What Would I Buy?* Homework Page.

Assessment

1. Use Assessment Indicators A3, A5, and A6 and the *Observational Assessment Record* to document students' abilities to solve addition problems using different strategies and to explain their reasoning.
2. Transfer appropriate documentation from the *Observational Assessment Record* to students' *Individual Assessment Record Sheets.*

Answer Key is on page 85.

Notes:

Student Guide (p. 65)

What Would I Buy?

Answers will vary.

Name _____ Date _____

What Would I Buy?

Homework

Dear Family Member:

Look at the items below with your child. Ask him or her to read the price for each item. Help your child with the reading of each question. Give your child pennies to help him or her decide which items to circle. To answer Question 2, your child could draw a picture or use a number sentence (for example, 5¢ + 3¢ = 8¢).

Thank you for your cooperation.

Look at the items below.

5¢   4¢   3¢   2¢

1. Circle the items you would buy if you had ten pennies. (If you want two of the same item, make two circles around it.)

2. How much would you pay for all the items you circled? Show how you found your answer.

    _____

3. Would you have any pennies left over? How many?

    _____

4. Make up a problem for other students to solve.

    _____

Purchasing with Pennies   SG • Grade 1 • Unit 3 • Lesson 7   65

Student Guide - page 65

Glossary

This glossary provides definitions of key vocabulary terms in the Grade 1 lessons. Locations of key vocabulary terms in the curriculum are included with each definition. Components Key: URG = *Unit Resource Guide* and SG = *Student Guide.*

A

Approximate (URG Unit 12)
1. (adjective) a number that is close to the desired number
2. (verb) to estimate

Area (URG Unit 10; SG Unit 12)
The amount of space that a shape covers. Area is measured in square units.

B

C

Capacity (URG Unit 9)
1. The volume of the inside of a container.
2. The largest volume a container can hold.

Circle (URG Unit 2)
A curve that is made up of all the points that are the same distance from one point, the center.

Circumference (URG Unit 15)
The distance around a circle.

Coordinates (URG Unit 19)
(In the plane) Two numbers that specify the location of a point on a flat surface relative to a reference point called the origin. The two numbers are the distances from the point to two perpendicular lines called axes.

Counting All (URG Unit 1)
A strategy for adding in which students start at one and count until the total is reached.

Counting Back (URG Unit 8)
A method of subtraction that involves counting from the larger number to the smaller one. For example, to find 8 − 5 the student counts 7, 6, 5 which is 3 less.

Counting On (URG Unit 1 & Unit 4)
A strategy for adding two numbers in which students start with one of the numbers and then count until the total is reached. For example, to count 6 + 3, begin with 6 and count three more, 7, 8, 9.

Counting Up (URG Unit 8)
A method of subtraction that involves counting from the smaller number to the larger one. For example, to find 8 − 5 the student counts 6, 7, 8 which is 3 more.

Cube (URG Unit 12 & Unit 15)
A solid with six congruent square faces.

Cubic Units (URG Unit 12)
A unit for measuring volume— a cube that measures one unit along each edge. For example, cubic centimeters and cubic inches.

cubic centimeter

Cylinder (URG Unit 15)
A three-dimensional figure with two parallel congruent circles as bases (top and bottom) and a curved side that is the union of parallel lines connecting corresponding points on the circles.

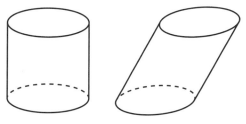

D

Data Table (URG Unit 3)
A tool for recording and organizing data on paper or on a computer.

Name	Age

Division by Measuring Out (URG Unit 14)
A type of division problem in which the number in each group is known and the unknown is the number of groups. For example, twenty students are divided into teams of four students each. How many teams are there? (20 students ÷ 4 students per team = 5 teams) This type of division is also known as measurement division.

Division by Sharing (URG Unit 14)
A type of division problem in which the number of groups is known and the unknown is the number in each group. For example, twenty students are divided into five teams. How many students are on each team? (20 students ÷ 5 teams = 4 students per team) This type of division is also known as partitive division.

E

Edge (URG Unit 15)
A line segment where two faces of a three-dimensional figure meet.

Equivalent Fractions (URG Unit 18)
Two fractions are equivalent if they represent the same part of the whole. For example, if a class has 8 boys and 8 girls, we can say $\frac{8}{16}$ of the students are girls or $\frac{1}{2}$ of the students are girls.

Even Number (URG Unit 4 & Unit 13)
Numbers that are doubles. The numbers 0, 2, 4, 6, 8, 10, etc. are even. The number 28 is even because it is 14 + 14.

F

Face (URG Unit 12 & Unit 15)
A flat side of a three-dimensional figure.

Fixed Variables (URG Unit 2, Unit 6 & Unit 11)
Variables in an experiment that are held constant or not changed. These variables are often called controlled variables.

G

H

Hexagon (URG Unit 2)
A six-sided polygon.

I

J

K

L

Length (URG Unit 6 & Unit 10)
1. The distance along a line or curve from one point to another. Distance can be measured with a ruler or tape measure.
2. The distance from one "end" to another of a two- or three-dimensional figure. For example, the length of a rectangle usually refers to the length of the longer side.

Line
A set of points that form a straight path extending infinitely in two directions.

Line Symmetry (URG Unit 7 & Unit 18)
A figure has line symmetry if it can be folded along a line so that the two halves match exactly.

Line of Symmetry (URG Unit 7 & Unit 18)
A line such that if a figure is folded along the line, then one half of the figure matches the other.

M

Making a Ten (URG Unit 13)
A strategy for adding and subtracting that takes advantage of students' knowledge of partitions of ten. For example, a student might find 8 + 4 by breaking the 4 into 2 + 2 and then using a knowledge of sums that add to ten.

$$8 + 4 =$$
$$8 + 2 + 2 =$$
$$10 + 2 = 12$$

Median (URG Unit 6 & Unit 9)
The number "in the middle" of a set of data. If there is an odd number of data, it is the number in the middle when the numbers are arranged in order. So the median of {1, 2, 14, 15, 28, 29, 30} is 15. If there is an even number of data, it is the number halfway between the two middle numbers. The median of {1, 2, 14, 15, 28, 29} is $14\frac{1}{2}$.

Mr. Origin (URG Unit 19)
A plastic figure used to help childen learn about direction and distance.

N

Near Double (URG Unit 13)
A derived addition or subtraction fact found by using doubles. For example, 3 + 4 = 7 follows from the fact that 3 + 3 = 6.

Number Sentence (URG Unit 3 & Unit 4)
A number sentence uses numbers and symbols instead of words to describe a problem. For example, a number sentence for the problem "5 birds landed on a branch. Two more birds also landed on the branch. How many birds are on the branch?" is 5 + 2 = 7.

O

Odd Number (URG Unit 4)
A number that is not even. The odd numbers are 1, 3, 5, 7, 9, and so on.

Origin (URG Unit 19)
A reference point for a coordinate system. If the coordinate system is a line, we can determine the location of an object on the line by the number of units it is to the right or the left of the origin.

P

Part (URG Unit 4)
One of the addends in part-part-whole addition problems.

Pattern Unit (URG Unit 7)
The portion of a pattern that is repeated. For example, AAB is the pattern unit in the pattern AABAABAAB.

Perimeter (URG Unit 6; SG Unit 12)
The distance around a two-dimensional shape.

Polygon
A closed, connected plane figure consisting of line segments, with exactly two segments meeting at each end point.

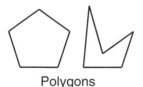
Polygons

Not Polygons

Prediction (URG Unit 5)
Using a sample to predict what is likely to occur in the population.

Prism (URG Unit 15)
A solid that has two congruent and parallel bases. The remaining faces (sides) are parallelograms. A rectangular prism has bases that are rectangles. A box is a common object that is shaped like a rectangular prism.

Q

Quadrilateral
A polygon with four sides.

R

Rectangle (URG Unit 2)
A quadrilateral with four right angles.

Rhombus (URG Unit 2)
A quadrilateral with four sides of equal length.

Rotational Symmetry (URG Unit 7)
A figure has rotational (or turn) symmetry if there is a point on the figure and a rotation of less than 360° about that point so that it "fits" on itself. For example, a square has a turn symmetry of $\frac{1}{4}$ turn (or 90°) about its center.

S

Sample (URG Unit 5)
Some of the items from a whole group.

Sphere (URG Unit 15)
A three-dimensional figure that is made up of points that are the same distance from one point, the center. A basketball is a common object shaped like a sphere.

Square (URG Unit 2)
A polygon with four equal sides and four right angles.

Symmetry (URG Unit 18)
(See Line Symmetry, Line of Symmetry, and Rotational Symmetry.)

T

Three-dimensional Shapes (URG Unit 15)
A figure in space that has length, width, and height.

TIMS Laboratory Method (URG Unit 5)
A method that students use to organize experiments and investigations. It involves four components: draw, collect, graph, and explore. It is a way to help students learn about the scientific method. TIMS is an acronym for Teaching Integrated Mathematics and Science.

Trapezoid (URG Unit 2)
A quadrilateral with exactly one pair of parallel sides.

Trial (URG Unit 6)
One attempt in an experiment.

Triangle (URG Unit 2)
A polygon with three sides.

Turn Symmetry
(See Rotational Symmetry.)

U

Using Doubles (URG Unit 13)
A strategy for adding and subtracting which uses derived facts from known doubles. For example, students use 7 + 7 = 14 to find that 7 + 8 is one more or 15.

Using Ten (URG Unit 13)
A strategy for adding which uses reasoning from known facts. For example, students use 3 + 7 = 10 to find that 4 + 7 is one more or 11.

V

Variable (URG Unit 2 & Unit 11)
A variable is something that varies or changes in an experiment.

Volume (URG Unit 9 & Unit 12; SG Unit 12)
1. The amount of space an object takes up.
2. The amount of space inside a container.

W

Whole (URG Unit 4)
The sum in part-part-whole addition problems.

X

Y

Z